Andrea welcomes the reader i..
practical devotional. She asks as many spiritual questions as she answers, allowing readers meditative space to consider God's presence and leading within their own lives. With scriptural guideposts, questions for reflection, and real-life illustrations, this devotional is a meaningful and worthwhile 12-week journey.

Rev. Dan Dzikowicz
Pastor & Organizational Consultant
dandzikowicz.com

Being FEARLESS does not come easily, nor is it supposed to, but Cladis insists that with reliance on Christ, we can develop resilience in all areas of our lives allowing us to face our demons and come out stronger than we ever thought possible. Cladis once again demonstrates her willingness is to be vulnerable with the reader, and her level of authenticity makes her work approachable and endearing. She freely offers up her struggles and shortcomings as tangible examples to help guide the reader through life's many challenges and speed bumps.

Cladis wants to be in that trench with us, so we can hear and know that despite doubt or failure, we can and will find a way to fearlessly move forward trusting in God's love and promise for our lives. Given my experience serving in ministry positions, I would highly recommend this devotional for anyone seeking steadfast accountability in their walk with Christ, for anyone who might doubt His promises, and most especially for younger adults needing a friend who is willing to tell not the convenient truths, but rather to prayerfully face up to the most difficult ones, while offering meaningful solutions. I will certainly revisit this devotional."

Ernelle LaCount
Former Children's Ministries Director
Calvary Church

Find Your Fearless!
Andrea G. Cladis

Put me in the game, coach! That's what I felt like saying after each week of the devotionals in *FEARLESS STRIDE*! Andrea takes you on a 12-week journey of the heart through her personal stories that point you directly toward Jesus. Deeply personal themes will resonate with everyone. Each week opens your heart more to Jesus and your own personal discovery and growth.

Through God's grace and love there is nothing we cannot overcome and endure. *FEARLESS STRIDE* challenges you to live the life God has designed for you. Discover and overcome what truly holds you back and allow this book to become your coach for 12 weeks! This devotional can help you get back in the game and know that God is leading you through any and all adversity and onward towards victory!

"Swing away" and bat down all your fears as you allow the fullness of God's grace to impact your heart through this 12-week devotional study.

Kari Scott
Founder of River Fitness Ministry
and Life's Little Blessings Book Club

FEARLESS STRIDE
FAITHFULLY RESILIENT IN CHRIST

A 12-Week Devotional

Fearless minds climb soonest unto crowns.
William Shakespeare, Henry VI

ANDREA CLADIS

Fearless Stride
Faithfully Resilient in Christ

ISBN: 978-0-578-49531-6
Copyright © 2019 Andrea Cladis

Published by Alive Publications
a division of
Alive Ministries: PROJECT PRAY
PO Box 1245
Kannapolis, NC 28082

www.alivepublications.org
www.projectpray.org

Holy Bible, King James Version, Cambridge, 1769.
Holy Bible, New International Version. Copyright: 1973, 1978, 1984
by International Bible Society, Zondervan Publishing House.

DEDICATION

This book is dedicated first and foremost to called third strikes. Yes, called third strikes, for they are my father, the fearless physician's, most loathed call in a baseball game. As my coach growing up, I knew from the look on Dad's face that striking out on a called third strike was perhaps the worst, most disappointment-inducing life decision I could make. But it's also what taught me that you can't stand around and wait for the perfect pitch in life. Sometimes you get a walk and sometimes you get hit-by-pitch, but most of the time, the pitch comes in fast, low and inside, and you can't stand there in fear, afraid to swing the bat while praying the umpire makes a call in your favor. I mean if you don't at least try to get on base, how can you ever start the journey towards home? The very least you can do is go down swinging and you should do it fearlessly, with a hint of swagger, because no matter what happens, God will always be there to dust you off and lead you home.

And thanks, Dad. For benching my siblings and me when we deserved it. For teaching us to be humble losers and gracious winners. Oh, and for the endless reminders to keep our eyes on the ball and swing the dang bat!

To the bullies I have known who challenged my confidence and made me tougher, to the runners who have crossed the finish line ahead of me, but encouraged me to keep moving, to the triathletes I have competed against, even the most aggressive one who used my lower body as a launching pad severely injuring my foot at the start of a race I still managed to finish, thank you for revealing the mental stamina within me I did not know I had. And to the 17-year-old me who wasn't running and wasn't fearless, I want you to know that we made it.

To the endless affirmations I have received from those whom I train in my exercise classes, I am thankful. Even though you often compare me to that which cannot be named, I am grateful you keep coming back to classes and fighting for a stronger, healthier YOU. It's okay if you think of me in fits of rage related to your delayed onset muscle soreness. Please know my sadistic smile is truly rooted in kindness for your progress.

And finally, to the future me and the future you, who will need to be reminded that even though life is scary and turbulent, maintaining your faith in God's eternal promise will provide you with the resilience you need to pick up the bat, step up to the plate, and refuse to go down without swinging. For the next 12 weeks, courage is required and called third strikes are not an option! But fearless strides most certainly are. So keep your eye on the ball and let's go ***PLAY BALL!***

CONTENTS

PART 1

WEEKS 1-4: FEARLESSLY BECOMING

PART 2

WEEKS 5-8: FAITHFULLY RESILIENT

PART 3

WEEKS 9-12: ETERNALLY OBEDIENT

PREFACE

What does it mean to be fearless in Christ?

In my first nonfiction book, Finding the Finish Line, I explored the idea that the ultimate aim in our lives should not be to chase some arbitrary finish line, but rather to move closer to Christ with each step that we take and each decision that we make. If our vital aim is closeness and intimacy in relationship with Christ, our lives will have abundant purpose and we will act in ways that glorify Christ and His kingdom. And because of God's grace, we can and should live out His plan for our lives fearlessly. God made the most enduring sacrifice for us and He counsels all believers not to be afraid, but to know that His mercy and love will abide in and around us. God is good today and always.

The goal of this book is to attempt to take the next step in understanding Christ and to answer the question of what it means to take "fearless strides" and what it means and looks like to live and be authentically fearless in Christ. To develop a sense of fearlessness, we first need to practice being resilient. Resilience can be defined as the capacity to recover with strength from difficulties. It is often equated with physical and mental toughness. It is not something that we are born with, but rather something we cultivate over time through life experiences. As the hardships of life shape us – anything from bullying to illness to job loss or the death of a loved one - we are forced to get back up again and to find renewal and purpose. We can let life sink us or we can find a new way to float, followed by an eagerness to swim forward. As I often say when speaking publicly, "You're either willing to grow or you're wanting to shrink." Resilience is as much about our attitude as it is about the circumstances in our lives that shape our thoughts, beliefs, and perspectives.

Life doesn't necessarily get easier as we grow older, but it always comes with an abundance of opportunities to develop purpose and to find meaning. In loss, we learn the depth of love and through suffering, we learn the courage of our character. Like a skin callous that hardens over time, resilience is an inner strength that helps us to endure through challenging times. The more difficulties we face, the more we grow and learn to adapt. And the more we adapt, the more we can bear and the quicker we can recover from the troubling situations that confront us in life.

Founder, chairman, and CEO of Life Time, Bahram Akradi describes balanced resilience as "continually putting one foot in front of the other and taking one step at a time, while being able to adjust the pace to handle what's in front of you at the moment." It is not always easy to achieve balanced resilience or to be resilient in general, but it is necessary for growth in our lives. Akradi explains that resiliency allows us to hang in there even when things get tough. It enables us to get to the other side where we will not only find new ways of being and existing, but we will create ways to thrive as individuals despite our circumstances. Life is certainly not a fair game we get to play, but the more resilient we become, the better equipped we will be to play it. Being resilient:

> "…can also teach us that we're strong and more capable than we ever thought possible…It can help us grow into more caring, compassionate, loving versions of ourselves. It can help us find deeper meaning and purpose in whatever comes next" *(Experience Life Magazine,* June 2018).

When I was in college, I recall having very little resilience. I was homesick much of my first year and my parents came to visit me often. I came home nearly every single weekend and I had no interest in facing my fears or learning to confront the difficulties I was confronting in a new and unfamiliar environment. Looking back, I missed an opportunity for growth that I did not embrace until my junior and senior year. Fear got in the way of my ability to be resilient, and I allowed it to cripple me.

However, I can now say with confidence, nearly fifteen years later, I have grown into adaptive fearlessness and progressive resilience. I have overcome an eating disorder that I no longer dwell on, I can finally sleep alone at night – which I was never able to do during my college days, and I have learned how to overcome the loss of pets and loved ones. I have endured injuries and setbacks both personally and professionally and I have found ways to cope with homesickness. I am confident in my faith and assured of victory through Christ. Being assured of His endless love has allowed me to find ways to be resilient and to know that I do not need to be afraid. I am not immune to pain. I am not sheltered from hardship. However, I have all the tools I need to be equipped to recover, to grow, and to learn through adverse experiences.

In my observations, I have found that we all share the following needs in order to feel a sense of security and contentment:

1. *A job or ministry* to sustain us.
2. *A safe place* to live.
3. *A person(s)* to love and to love us in return.

Each of these needs we possess feeds and fuels the others. If we feel emptiness or lack of satisfaction in one of these areas, we will over-compensate by trying to grow the others to fill in the gap. For this reason, people may become workaholics or develop an addiction to porn or physical pleasuring instead of finding satisfaction in true love. They may become obsessive-compulsive in the organization of their home space or they may become hoarders or forever roommates or become apt to develop another unsavory habit that displeases God. None of these distractions or 'gap-fillers' serve to advance God's purpose and the Kingdom of Heaven.

Yet, with that in mind, there's a strong chance that having all three things in balance at the same time in our life might not always happen. Maybe we get two out of three, or one out of three, or none at all, depending on what is happening in our lives. Perhaps we lose a job or are longing for love, or our family is broken or we no longer have one. Regardless of circumstance, God calls upon us to trust in Him and to know that He alone can and will fulfill us. God has given us life and God has a divine plan for our hearts to serve Him.

If you consider the short list above and replace the italic phrases with **God**, the revised list of what it is we need to be fulfilled and to be fearless is quite remarkable:

1. GOD to sustain us.
2. GOD to live.
3. GOD to love and to love us in return.

It takes faith to be fearless. It takes resilience. It takes heart and resolute bravery. So, where do we begin? How can we recognize the work of God in us and practice fearlessness in our lives?

Journey through this 12-week devotional series and discover renewed courage to live the life that God has called you to! Learn how to tackle adversity through the right attitude, to embody grace while also having grit, and to be courageous even in the face of failure or loss.

Each section of this devotional provides you with a focus for the week, questions to ponder, prayer to pursue, and action steps for you to outline the ways you will actively practice being fearless and resilient in your life so that you draw closer to Christ and invite others to experience the joy and redemption that He provides. For each action step, write down concrete ideas for making improvements in your life. Be intentional with your reflection on each weekly focus point and try to set yourself up to experience tangible changes in your life that move you closer to Christ and further away from fear.

Utilize this devotional as an opportunity to instigate forward movement in your life and in the lives of those around you. Allow your attitudes to become your actions and your perception of life in Christ to be vibrantly transformed. Everyone has fears, but remember that even in those fears, God is by our side, holding our hands, and wanting to breathe new life into the delicate work of our hearts.

Go forth and be fearless! Trust in God's loving plan for your life. Do not give up on His grace or His mercy. You are sheltered in His perfect love. You deserve to live this life with purpose as you draw near to the Lord your God. Your heavenly creator made you for a reason!

*It is time to move closer to Christ
and further away from fear.*

He has saved us and called us to a holy life – not because of anything we have done, but because of his own purpose and grace. This grace was given us in Christ Jesus before the beginning of time (2 Timothy 1:9).

Fearlessly Becoming

As you begin this 12-week series, the most significant challenge you have is to love yourself, have grace upon yourself, and to trust that God has you planted exactly where he wants you to be. In all stages of life, we are becoming. Think about that for a moment. Each of us is a work in progress. God is always working in us and through us. Maybe you are becoming a mother, a wife, a husband or a father. Maybe you are becoming a renewed person on account of new career interests or passions, maybe you are becoming a more engaged citizen or community member. Maybe you are a creator working on a piece of art or maybe you are becoming a caretaker for parents or a more determined devotee of your friends or family. Whatever it is, I hope you are in the position of embracing new perspectives in relation to the world around you.

Regardless of the how or the why, wherever you are in your life, you are in a position to become the fearless person whom God created. Some days you might feel like you are right on track, you are hitting the mark, you are doing all you can and becoming all you can be. Yet, some days, the reality will be that the painful or discomforting parts of growth and becoming are not all that pleasant. You may even feel as though you are regressing or unbecoming who God wants you to be. But even on those days and during those discouraging seasons that do not feel rewarding, remember that God is still using you! He is still shaping you as His child and working through you for the glory of His eternal purpose.

To fearlessly become who God intends you to be, you have to trust, listen, act, and react. Leading a Christian life is not a passive act. It is a daily decision to love others, to serve your community, and to share the Gospel of Christ. You can most certainly spitefully

ignore God's call, but that will lead to unhappiness and discontent-
ment. However, if you choose to listen, if you choose to follow God's
lead, if you choose to lean in and cherish His love for you, each day
you will take new strides towards accepting His plan for your life and
becoming a more faithful steward for His kingdom.

The year I originally began writing this devotional, my personal
memoir came out. I recall many tears during the process of writing it
and the countless evenings I spent shredding the pages I had written recalling painful memories about trauma and heartbreak. Draw-
ing strength from courage nestled deep within my soul, the acceptance for publication of my memoir was gratifying. However, when
my memoir was finally released into the world, I cried yet again. But
those tears were not like the tears I cried during the difficult process of writing it. They were tears of catharsis, growth, and spiritual
renewal. I no longer felt weary or vulnerable in the recollection of
my past experiences because I was finally able to see how God was
using my personal agony and example of faith to reach others. I will
never forget the moment when I closed my eyes, smiling through
my tears, cradling my nearly 400-page heart-wrenching memoir in
hand, resolutely understanding that through God's persistent work
in me, I had become fearlessly brave enough to go forth and share
my story.

Hustle & Hardship

Is the hustle worth the hardship?

A brisk early November wind blew the decay of wet, fallen leaves towards my face as I walked in the misty rain to the starting line of an annual eight-mile fall race called "The Hot Cider Hustle."

For me, races act as symbolic placeholders in a given month and a given year. They mark a new season of training and the steady passage of time. Summers mean hot weather, triathlons and cycling events; fall means cooler weather, marathons and longer endurance races. Winter means snowclad running friends and closed trails; spring means warming weather, short races, light rains, dampened trails with new undergrowth and sneezing fits, which come as consequence of the fresh foliage coming to life.

The Hot Cider Hustle always found its place on the calendar nestled between my last fall marathon and the final biking event I participated in each autumn season. It marked the end of the racing season and acted as the official transition to colder months and much needed time off from long outdoor training sessions. It was the placeholder on the calendar that willed me to embrace one last rush of running freedom before the busy holiday season and icy anticipation of a new year. In many ways, it made me nostalgic that another year and race season had passed, and in other ways, the race made me feel proud of all I had accomplished. I was usually happy to give my legs a break from the grind of constant preparatory training.

The first time I ran the Hot Cider Hustle, my Dad went with me and cheered me on every time I emerged from the heavily wooded forest setting of the race. The second year I experienced the race, I had just started a new job the month prior. The third-year racing, my mom had new health complications that had riled my family. The fourth year, I was beginning a relationship with my future spouse and had invited him to attend. He got frostbitten waiting for me at the finish line, but I remember feeling happy he was there. I told him to wear a warmer jacket the following year. He took that as a sign we would still be together in a year's time and soon the frigid temps no longer seemed to bother him. New love certainly makes one say and do untenable things.

The following year, however, I did not make it to the race. My four-year-old dog, Kody, tragically passed away the evening before the race from a rare form of cancer. He had fought one heck of a battle to stay alive as long as he did. I know he only did it for us. He suffered tremendously. The year after his death I chose not to attend the race as the memory association with Kody's death was far too raw. But, time can heal wounds, or in the very least, death and grief can provide a necessary momentum to keep us wanting to live our best lives for as long as we are able. Two years after Kody passed, and following a long hiatus from recreational running, I was more determined than ever to return to the race and to prove that I could run again. I wanted to run for Kody, for myself, for my love of the fall season, and for the strength of pushing through a collective challenge with strangers who would become friends by the time we crossed the finish line.

On the precipice of a new year, I would graduate with my Master of Fine Arts in Writing and also attain my "MRS." Degree. The planned race marked a turning point and transition in my life. I was attempting to overcome the haunting memory of my physically crippled young dog. I was also trying to process what it would be like to start a new job with a new degree and take on the role of a wife and maybe one day, a mother. I was scared, but I was also determined. I knew the pace I set during that race would have an impact on the pace of the rest of the current year and the year ahead. I had to be strong and I knew I had to race fearlessly.

It began as a morning like many other race mornings I had experienced in my life. I woke up early, tried on several outfits, only to end up wearing what I had initially chosen the previous night. I said a prayer for a safe, injury-free racing experience and I practiced a few visualization strategies. Visualizing the performance of a given activity provides the opportunity to see yourself to and through a successful execution of whatever it is you seek to accomplish. Visualization for a race lets me see myself outside of my body, observe my pace, check off completion of each mile, and cross that finish line! It also helps to alleviate the many nerves that accompany any race. No matter how long or short the race, it is both a mental and physical activity requiring stamina and endurance, especially when Mother Nature does her very best to hinder personal efforts.

During the Hot Cider Hustle of 2017, she did her very best to make it a race I will not soon forget. There was a warning about potentially severe weather. And while imminent thunderstorms and subsequent flooding had been prevalent in the forecast, they were considered questionable and the race had not been canceled. After all, the eager runners had paid their fees and they wanted to run their race! It was time for them to cash in on the recreational experience they had patiently waited for. I was one of those overly exuberant, ambitious runners. Despite warnings from my father and mother about the weather conditions, I was not going to stay in bed and miss the opportunity to set foot on the trail in this particular autumn race. I did not want to wait another year to get out there and tackle this course. It would serve as a sort of psychological victory for me and that would be far more gratifying than any kind of physical pain the race would deal me.

Layered in clothing consisting of long-sleeve Under Armour, fleece-lined leggings, two pairs of socks, a winter hat, a running vest, and a purple and white waterproof (or so it claimed) windbreaker, I set out into the misty rain and bone-chilling wind to the starting line of the Hot Cider Hustle. The race pack was much slimmer than I had remembered in previous years. Many runners had made the arguably wise decision to cut their losses and stay warm and dry in bed!

But, the rest of the crazy, bundled-up runners who had decided to get out of bed waited at the starting cue to begin the journey. The race, set in a densely wooded forest traversed eight miles of gravel, mud, and grass-covered hills. To me, it was the most beautiful race of the fall season. However, this particular race year, it ended up being rather treacherous. The first mile went smoothly. I was cold but was keeping a steady pace and warming up. I was listening to Christian music and it was keeping me calm and focused. Entering mile number two, I began thinking maybe, just maybe we will make it through this race before the storms come. But to my luck, moments after that thought crossed my mind, we all heard the first crack of thunder and witnessed three ambient flashes of lightning. The clouds began swirling above us and the small amount of light that had filtered through them dissipated. A few sprinkles came down from the clouds and then within no more than two minutes, the skies opened and released the heaviest rains I have witnessed in my life. Mixed with hail, the deluge didn't spare any runner. Soon enough, visible bruising was noticed on the legs of the runners who were wearing shorts. People were covering their heads with their hands and water bottles and desperately seeking shelter from the storm. Some runners dodged heavy hail by ducking underneath low tree branches. Others called out for their friends to form a protective huddle.

CRACK! RIPPLE! *FLASH!*

The entirety of mile number three was filled with the cacophony of nature's cleansing tantrum. I whimpered a little as my music stopped. The speakers had flooded with water. My water-logged socks and shoes felt clunky and heavier with each stride. I trudged through the puddles that were growing bigger with each step as visibility significantly decreased. All of that visualizing the night before was not panning out as anticipated.

Mile number four brought more rain, and an eerie morning light that peered through the clouds. I became discouraged with my progress. I wanted to return home and escape the awful decision I had made to run into this forest during such a vicious autumn storm. I prayed that the rains would subside. I scrubbed eyes to alleviate the stinging feel of the water pelting against my face. I removed the hood from my "waterproof" jacket as it was no use to me. All it did was trap more icy water around the nape of my neck. I looked ahead of me and behind me. I was isolated from the other small groups of runners. Many were stopping to seek some type of shelter, but none was to be found.

Mile five finally came. Sirens were blaring, signaling us off of the course. Unfortunately, the only way out was to finish the race. I wanted to cry. Instead, I hummed a tune to myself to drown out my fear of the approaching thunder. *Just keep running, just keep running*, I told myself. The popular animated fish named Nemo could literally swim through this! *Just keep running, just keep running!* Lost in the trail of my distracting thoughts on account of the discomfort of my physical condition, I began thinking about Jesus and the trials he faced as a servant of God. Though I was still literally being pelted from wet, cold rain on all sides, I felt warm in that moment of thinking about Jesus and my God. I thought of His unshakable courage and the fearless nature of his mission on earth. He was fearless because he was perfectly loved by the God who never fails us. The word "fearless" continued to resonate with me. *Fearless*, I thought. *Be fearless. In every stride, be fearless.*

Entering the sixth mile of the race, the rainy mix turned to hail the size of plump grapes. It felt as though someone was throwing ice pellets from the sky. The winds increased in velocity and I pushed forward. About halfway through the mile, sliding on the wet leaves, I was no longer able to feel the harshness of the cold. I let a slight smile creep onto my face. The runners ahead were surprisingly still moving. The stragglers behind me continued to press forward. I was a solitary runner snuggled between the two groups. It was a strangely good place to be. I was not leading, nor was I following from behind. I was running my own race and I was doing it fearlessly. If I had died in that forest, I would have been content if that were God's will. However, if I made it through, which I believed I would, I knew that would be a result of His deliverance and protection.

The seventh mile of the race seemed to come up rather quickly. The hail gradually morphed into a steady rain and the winds let up their burgeoning wrath. I continued to whelm my thoughts in prayer. I continued to upgrade my will to be fearless. I ran with my eyes closed for about 200 meters and soon enough, mile marker eight was visible. I knew I was going to make it! I picked up the pace of my stride to the best of my ability. I was coming off of a gnarly foot injury that had sidelined me most of the summer, so I did not want to push my luck. It was wet, slick, dangerous, and I did not need to be injured again or aggravate my past injury. It was not worth the risk to me. Plenty of runners had wiped out, but most of them had quickly gotten back in the race! There was a strong element of resilience on display that day. We were all going to make it to that finish line no matter how long it took to get there. It would be a well-deserved victory for each and every one of us. It would undoubtedly result in slower racing times and maybe, in the realization that it was not the best decision of our lives to run that race. Nevertheless, we would finish with renewed strength and determination – the kind of determination that only comes out of personal struggle, out of some intolerable challenge that forces one to overcome.

As I reflect on this race, I believe that much of life is striving, doing our best to be in condition for an unpredictable race. We get caught in storms for which we cannot plan and in order to get through them we have to keep running. The run may not get easier, and the rain may become colder and physically bruising, but we have to be fearless in order to survive. Each step was more miserable than the last, but I kept moving on. The only way out was to keep running.

The sirens crescenoded in their warning to clear the course, but leaving the path would mean being lost in a rain-soaked forest in the middle of a torrential downpour. Staying on the path and following it to the finish was the only option.

As I was trying to distract myself from misery, I continued thinking about how life is that storm-drenched colorful forest in the fall. Slippery leaves, erratic winds, wet, cold, bone-chilling, and dark. There remained a little hint of where the path led and there was no option to turn back. We run and we keep running. We go through darkness and we feel alone. It is in this wet, cold, scary place that we have only one option and that is to find fearlessness within us. We must be resolute in our final aim to win and to conquer.

I finally made it to the muddy pit of a 400-meter stretch of the old horse racing track that served as the last part of the racecourse. I thought about the song, "We Win" from the Christian music group, *MercyMe*. The song speaks to the reality that no matter what happens in life – no matter what trials or adversity we face – in the end, we win! We win because our salvation is in Christ! We have the grace and mercy of His great love. We win because he has already won for us! With a few proud fist pumps and a winning attitude, I plowed through the rest of the muddy track as the rains finally began to dissipate. 300 meters, 200, 100, and 50 to finish. I lost both of my shoes in the mud, but I kept running until I crossed that finish line. "We win!" I shouted. "We win!" Every single one of the runners that finished before me and after me in that race had won something. Perhaps they were not thinking of heaven's eternal glory, but they won in victory over the present obstacle. And that is how we have to go about our lives, one rainy stride at a time until we reach the glory of the finish line.

My dad graciously greeted me at the finish. I was visibly shaking and my lips were blue. My legs were chaffed from the wet fabric of my pants and my body was completely caked in mud. Dad wrapped me a towel and we sipped some hot cider. Okay, I gulped down the warmth of the cider. Lots of cider. I began to feel a bit nauseous, but the cider was warm. I wanted to drink myself full of it. My dad held onto me as I leaned into him and after we ambled to the shelter of our car, he helped me put on some dry clothing. He came to my rescue as he always had. He applauded my resilience and offered to get me food and a hot shower, both of which I craved at that moment. I realized as I watched him act in self-sacrifice on my behalf that I was fearless in that race not because I wasn't scared. I mean, I was. There was a lot of rain and lightning, thunder and hail with a high probability of injury out on the course. Yet, the real reason I was fearless was that I knew love awaited me on the other side of the finish line. I was fearless because I knew I was loved by my father on Earth and my Father in Heaven. Whether we are shaking off the heavy rains of an eight-mile race or not, in life, we must remind ourselves that we are always running into His arms knowing that in the end, He will deliver us. We can be fearless in our daily stride because this race we run, this path we are on, this life we live, has already been won. He has conquered all things and He remains the victor for us today and for all eternity. Yes! *We win!*

> *I have told you these things, so that in me you may have peace. In this world you will have trouble. But take heart! I have overcome the world* (John 16:33).

TRAIN. CONNECT. PRAY.

How will you **train** for Christ and His Kingdom today?
How will you **connect** with others today?
How will you **pray** today?

DEVOTIONAL INQUIRY:

1. **Train:** What resonated with you from this section about "Hustle and Hardship?"

_____

_____

_____

2. **Connect:** How does this message connect to your own personal hardships? How does the thought of being fearless change your mindset regarding challenges, goals, hopes, and dreams?

_____

_____

_____

3. **Pray:** How will you pray today? What is the conversation you need to be having with God?

_____

_____

_____

DATE: _____

GRACE IN RESILIENCE SCALE (1-10; 1 being low resilience, 10 being highly resilient): _____

OUTLINE your action plan for _prayer, connection, and training_ in relation to "Hustle & Hardship."

_____

_____

_____

Devotional Prayer

Heavenly Father,

Thank you for your consistent provision for me through all the storms of this life. Thank you for equipping me with the strength I need to face adversity and to conquer my fears. By remaining in your word, I am able to surrender myself to the comfort of your love and grace. This life you have given me to live is an exciting journey and I am grateful that I get to explore the way you unveil new beauty to me each and every day.

Lord, when I feel defeated, please help me look up to you. When I feel afraid or have lost my way, please remind me of your presence. Lord, I promise today and always to run fearlessly for you, your mercy, and your promise of eternal life. Even when the skies turn gray and I have lost my way, I will trust your hand to lead me home. Thank you for guiding me to your truths and helping me to remain in you. For the reminder of your steadfast love in all things and the gift of relational intimacy with you, I seek to praise your name.

Lord God, let the race I run serve as an example to others of what it looks like to run towards you with a trusting heart, assured of the glory of the yet unseen finish line. I promise to hustle towards you no matter what the hardship.

In your holy name, I pray.

Amen.

Freedom & Failure

What would Jesus do?

When confronted with additional freedoms and new responsibilities, we occasionally succumb to failure in the most important task we have, which is to serve Christ and His Kingdom in all things. We too often fail to exercise discipline, restraint, and self-control. Embracing unbounded freedom, we are distracted. Too much freedom can be detrimental to the improvement of our lives. It can lead to personal failure or our waning ability to put our best selves forward to serve God. On the other hand, freedom can also provide new opportunities to experience God's love and creatively act upon our desire to serve Him and those around us. Freedom is a good thing and, in many ways, accepting failure can also be positive. In the end, it is our job to recognize our failures, acknowledge our freedoms, and act upon both responsibly.

In the early 90s, cloth bracelets that read, "W.W.J.D" (What Would Jesus Do?) were trendy and popular. My youth group friends wore them and so did my non-church going friends. I loved their multitude of colors. I liked wearing them as a way of sharing my faith while also having an item of jewelry that helped me feel like I fit in with the crowd. I wore a W.W.J.D. bracelet for as long as I can remember. I never took it off. Through swim meets and softball games, family road trips, barbeques, and messy baking sessions with my mom. That bracelet was a daily reminder to me of the question, "What would Jesus do?" In any given situation, that question was worth pursuing. *"What would Jesus do?"* When my very first purple W.W.J.D. bracelet broke due to its frayed edges, I cried for nearly two hours. I thought it was a sign from God that I was failing him or I was making decisions of which Jesus would not approve. While that might have been somewhat true, more likely, my sensitivity might have been a result of my childhood innocence, I am not completely sure. What I do know is that I took the bracelet and its question seriously, even at a young age. I am glad that I had that experience of self-evaluation through the lens of Christian moral values. My mom did buy me a new teal and white bracelet a few days later. Thankfully, my childlike hope was restored. Nevertheless, the point is that the question is valid, especially when we confront freedom and free will. I think the WWJD question allows us to evaluate our lives. In our freedom, we don't have to fail God. But we do need to ask what God wants us to do. What personal endeavor, creation, or collective activity will draw us closer to Him?

Reflect on this idea of being pushed towards and pulled away from Christ and what influences in your life pull you near or push you away from God. Ask the daily question, "What would Jesus do?" It could help improve your attitude about an undesirable task at work or give you the courage to stand up for yourself. It may even afford you the humility to perform an act of service you otherwise would not have done. It is a worthy question. *What would Jesus do?*

Romans 12:2 guides us through this fragile balance between freedom, failure, and the temptations of the world. "Do not conform to the pattern of this world, but be transformed by the renewing of your mind. Then you will be able to test and approve what God's will is--his good, pleasing, and perfect will." The word "transform" is one of the most thought-provoking words in all of scripture. As we believe in Christ, we are transformed and we are made new. We renew our minds through him, dismissing the influences of the outside world. We are transformed in a remarkable way. When we allow ourselves to see Christ fully, and we open ourselves up to the wonder of His loving guidance for our lives, we no longer need to seek short-term fulfillment in worldly pleasures or temptations.

A SHIFTING PARADIGM

In 2017, I wrote my family's Christmas letter as a reflection on our digitally saturated, heavily distracted world. It read a little something like this:

Yuletide greetings, compliments of an eccentric writer and the crazy Cladis clan!

Last year around this time, I got a notification that Christ was born. I rubbed my eyes and looked twice at the digital device telling me of the birth of my Lord and Savior. I did not know what to do. Was it true? Was I to make a post or tweet or meme of the news I had received? As I weighed my options, I decided I wanted the world to know. I wanted to tell everyone, but in so doing, I did not connect the message of Christ or His birth with anyone. The more I pondered the compelling notification of the birth of Christ, the more I realized the opportunity I had and have in my everyday life to tell others of the good news of Christ. But telling people through social media or through some channel within our digital world is not the way to reach people. You don't win hearts through text messages or persuasive posts about your beliefs. You don't win hearts through seeking validation for what it is you believe.

You win hearts through time spent in the presence of another. You win hearts by showing the love of Christ to others. You win hearts through love, acceptance, compassion, and care. You win hearts by putting the phone down and listening to the person right in front of you. As Christians, we should strive to win hearts for Christ. To allow others to witness the beauty of His love, His sacrifice, and the Kingdom of Heaven He has prepared for us.

I have spent the past semester of graduate school studying the effects of digital media and communications on the way people interact with each other, learn new skills, express themselves, conduct business, and relate to the world without physically having to connect with anyone.

The decorative title of my research thesis, designed to make me sound smart and pretentious, of which I am and am not, is *A SHIFTING*

PARADIGM: An Evaluation of the Pervasive Effects of Digital Technologies on Language Expression, Creativity, Critical Thinking, Political Discourse, and Interactive Processes of Human Communications.

Throughout my extensive research, I discovered a lot about how our world is changing due to digital technologies; it is changing at a rapid pace. Our brains are being re-wired to facilitate expedited processing. Children are growing up as digital natives knowing nothing of a former "analog" world. Our capacity for memory is failing as we participate in cognitive offloading activities, and we are losing the ability to converse naturally with others around us. Further, we are craving things that bring us towards more mindful behaviors because we no longer know what it means to be present, and we are slowly becoming passive, complacent receivers of information rather than proactive, creative, innovators of new knowledge.

I could go on about what I have learned and if you're interested, feel free to check out the following publication: https://journals.sagepub.com/eprint/hkZWxD9MAxUpxgqZyxuc/full. But in the meantime, consider the following questions and think about that notification of Jesus Christ being born showing up on your newsfeed.

How does our digital dependency affect our consumption, use, and understanding of language and the world around us? What can we forecast as the cumulative results of our behaviors in the digital age? If we cannot connect with others outside of the virtual reality in which we can so easily exist or if we cannot debate or sustain meaningful discourse without the interruption of digital technologies, can we ever become rational, self-functioning, thinking, human beings again?

Aside from all of the components of my research, an overarching theme that I have unveiled seems obvious – with or without the need for research – yet it appears to be widely ignored. And that simple theme is that in our growing digital world, we are lacking connection with others. We are lacking the intimacy of conversation, the warmth of human touch, the provision of a support system that presents itself outside of digital networks.

Think about this. Can you imagine if the birth of Christ was first revealed as a post on social media? "Weighing in at 6.2 pounds, 22 inches long, the proud, but humble parents, Joseph and Mary thank you for your support at this time…"

And then soon enough some wise man takes to twitter, snaps a picture of some worn-out donkey, berates Joseph as not being the biological Father, reveals the claim that this newborn infant is the son of God, and all-too-suddenly the birth goes viral, people are posting comments, videos and unfounded chatter ensues. People swarm the stable, there is conflict around the manger, Joseph goes on the defense to protect his wife and son, and then cameras flood the scene, news crews make their appearance, and late-night talk show hosts laugh at the meager birth of a little boy who is labeled "Jesus." Imagine the chaos. Imagine the doubts. Imagine the sheer magnitude of disrespect and criticism that would have been in store for some virgin woman giving birth in Bethlehem.

Thankfully, though, his birth did not happen in the vapid space of a digitally connected world. There was certainly great trial and adversity, but his birth happened in a moment of silence, peace, and the innocence of humble birth. The wise men who came did not follow hashtags or tweets to arrive on the scene, they followed the brilliance of the stars in the night sky. And they came not with comments on posts or emojis showing excitement, they came with gold, incense, myrrh, and gratefulness in their hearts.

Think of that silent stillness. Where can you find it in your life today? Where can you locate that quiet peace? Where do you see those everyday miracles? What is the uncommon moment of this past year that you cling to for hope and salvation?

My prayer is that you will stop long enough to find it. Even if it is just in the moment of reading Christmas letters or correspondence still sent by snail mail from friends and family. I suppose if I really wanted to prove my point, I would have handwritten this letter. Yet, I am not immune to the digital world. I, too, have realized how connected I am to others and the world via cyberspaces and not physical ones. I was recently reminded by a leader at my church that our most valuable commodity in this world is relational time. But we allow our lives to be consumed by other things for the sake of income gathering, efficiency, and this idea that doing more will produce better outcomes for our lives. I fall victim to this fallacy nearly every day. However, time with God and the moments spent with others that we can hold onto are the things in this world that ultimately matter. So, disconnect, unplug, and recharge not your device, but your soul.

I cannot claim to know what humanity needs. But *what would Jesus do?* I think He would tell us to take pause. I do think we need fewer machines and devices and more physical touch and intentional friendships. I do think we need fewer social media and more tech time outs. I do think we need to see God in the world more. We need to see His presence and experience Him not through a device, an app, or post. We need to create quiet silence and stillness to be aware of His presence in our lives.

Seek to find that quiet at Christmas and throughout the year. Hold onto a moment and create a memory without a selfie. Embrace God – in both freedom and failure - and feel his arms hugging the world and gathering it up in the warmth and promise of what He provides in eternity for us.

Fight the good fight of faith. Take hold of the eternal life to which you were called when you made your good confession in the presence of many witnesses (1 Timothy 6:12).

TRAIN. CONNECT. PRAY.

How will you **train** for Christ and His Kingdom today?
How will you **connect** with others today?
How will you **pray** today?

DEVOTIONAL INQUIRY:

1. **Train:** What resonated with you from this section about "Freedom & Failure?" How can we honor God with the freedom that we have? How can we move closer to him in our failures?

   _____

   _____

   _____

2. **Connect:** How can you connect this discussion and inquiry about digital communications to your everyday life? Do digital technologies get in the way of your quiet time with Christ or have you found ways to implement technology as a complement to your time with God? List a few ways that you can proactively engage with Christ and others apart from technology?

   _____

   _____

   _____

3. **Pray:** How will you pray today? What is the conversation you need to be having with God?

   _____

   _____

   _____

DATE: _____

GRACE IN RESILIENCE SCALE (1-10): _____

OUTLINE your action plan for _prayer, connection, and training_ in relation to "Freedom & Failure."

_____

_____

_____

Devotional Prayer

Heavenly Father,

Help me to be more focused on your word and work in my life. I am sorry for allowing digital distractions to get in the way of furthering my relationship with you. I ask for forgiveness as I know that the allure of instant gratification has kept me from fully pursuing you.

Thank you for the blessing that technology is in the lives of so many people around the world. I praise you that we can connect to others in new ways, disperse knowledge, create ideas, and most importantly we can also utilize the common digital space as a platform to share your word and spread the Gospel.

Lord God, I pray that you will use me as an instrument for your good and that I will learn to use technology to serve your kingdom and not to hide from it. Help me to always keep my eyes on you and not merely on a screen full of distractions.

In your holy name I pray.

Amen.

Attitude & Adversity

*How does your attitude shape
your response to adversity?*

One of the many doctors in my family recently asked me, "What is it that you do?"

Apparently being an artist and a teacher seems ethereal when compared to the practice of medicine. I think it really comes down to an understanding of the differences between the sciences and the arts. That's not a conversation for this book, but surprisingly, the "What do you do on a daily basis in your job?" is a question I get rather often, not only from doctors or folks with traditional careers. It's a common inquiry since we too often define others by what they do rather than by who they are. Sometimes I get offended as though invalidated by their query. At other times, I just accept the common misunderstandings that we share.

The doctor said to me, "I diagnose, treat, problem-solve, and prescribe medications for healing. What is it that you do?"

I, the artist, replied, "I, too, diagnose, problem solve, and create avenues for healing. I make visible what is invisible. I write prescriptions for the human spirit."

The doctor reacted with the following statement: "Perhaps it isn't just the body which needs healing." He is correct in his observation. It is not just the body which needs healing, but rather the whole self that needs healing. Our minds, emotions, spirits, and sense of being in this world are all in need of some form of restorative healing. Doctors are healers, but then again, so are artists and anyone seeking to do the work of Christ here on earth.

I include this brief exchange here because I think it serves as a powerful reminder that no matter what we do – whether it is working in a technical field, medical field, participating in the creation of arts, or serving as a caretaker for friends or family - we all play a role in serving others while shaping and caring for the common humanity we share. As an artist, I admittedly struggle to accept the reality that what I do has value. Many artists do not make much money and what they produce acquires a sense of value to the receiver that is more often intangible than tangible. Thus, I wrestle with embracing the fact that my work does help others to experience the world differently or reveal to them new avenues towards curative wellness and meaning in their lives.

Sometimes I, too, get caught up in the mindset that I must be *doing* and *achieving* in terms of measurable outcomes rather than qualitative ones. If the big paycheck is not there and I did not physically save a life through a medical miracle, does that mean I, as a person, carry any less value than those who do perform those things? Then again, if I take an alternative perspective, maybe my words have saved a life, or my work as a fitness trainer has given people a new source or second chance at life. No one has compensated me in the way of the doctors of this world, but regardless of what society might want me to believe, I do not need that sort of definitive remuneration to know I am doing what God has placed me on this Earth to do! As an artist, I get to be a translator of God's beauty here on earth, and that in and of itself is a gift. Remember, *"Whatever it is that you do, work at it with all your heart...It is the Lord Christ you are serving"* (Colossians 3:23-24).

In regard to taking those fearless strides as a creator, despite pending adversity, it is crucial to remember that God is the greatest creator! He is the original Creator and our fearless Creator. He made us perfectly and beautifully and He wants us to live the life He has given us using the gifts He has bestowed upon us. How profoundly powerful is this life-giving reality that the greatest creator wants us to be fearless in the pursuit of His will for our lives? So, what if I am an artist? What if I experience life differently than the doctor or the lawyer? Does that mean that what I contribute to this world has any less value? Should I succumb to societal stereotypes or should I relish in the beauty of God's design for my life?

Widely revered psychologist, Mihaly Csikszentmihalyi, said the following after more than 30 years of observing creative people:

> If I had to express in one word what makes their personalities different from others, it's complexity. They show tendencies of thought and action that in most people are segregated. They contain contradictory extremes; instead of being an individual, each of them is a multitude... Perhaps this is why creative people are so difficult to pin down. In both their creative processes and their brain processes, they bring seemingly contradictory elements together in unusual and unexpected ways.

When I reflect upon Mihaly's observations, I feel somewhat justified in the mode of being through which I operate in life. I like structure, but I also thrive on chaos. I like to have answers, but I prefer exploring the unknown. I crave security, but I am driven by the chase towards that which does not guarantee a predictable outcome. I have long been called a 'complex' person and there are always competing components of my personality and thinking processes that present themselves on a daily basis. As a result of these tendencies of my persona, I struggle emotionally in many life circumstances, and I am constantly hungry to create and to achieve. However, my driving desires do not always expose themselves in anticipated patterns. I feel things deeply and have a strong connection to what is happening around me. It is easy for me to feel lost in a world of incessant movement and it is hard for me to feel comfortable as a creative in a world that demands instantaneous results.

As such, it is important to focus not on tangible results, but on personal ingenuity. I must embrace my creative side, despite the naysayers who dismiss it as folly, while also tempering its scattered tendencies with the reality that Christ is steadfast. He does not waver. He is not contradictory. He will not reject me or see me as any less worthy because I am *His* creation. I AM HIS CHILD. I often remind myself that He made me the way I am for a reason. He made me a creator. I will say it again. He made me in His perfect image. We are all made with gifts that we can and should use to glorify Him and bring others to Christ. The test of balancing order and chaos in our lives will forever be present. Yet, with the right attitude about both who we are and how God has called us and gifted us to function – as doctors, artists, engineers, homemakers, musicians, athletes, entrepreneurs, etc. - we can all face adversity with a fearless attitude and in turn, respond to God's call for our lives with an aura of eternal joy and contentment.

Another example of confronting attitude and adversity can be found in our physical desire to attain a goal. As I am writing this, my wrists are quivering and the muscles in my upper arms and shoulders are twitching. My boxing coach put me through a heck of a workout and I am still feeling the residual effects. The aforementioned workout consisted of stimulating rhythmic patterns of punches, including jabs, hooks, uppercuts and power punches. In each round I completed, I struggled to keep up with the speed at which my coach wanted me to hit. Throughout each round, he called out directives for punches and told me to hit harder, faster, and with more strength on each sequential hit. He told me to dig deep and to not back down. Motivated to meet his standards, I obliged. And in the fury of my arm movements, torso-twisting, sweat-dripping, heavy breathing dizziness, I felt a surge of freedom.

As fatigue set in and numbness was felt throughout my tingling body, I realized that all of the worries and stressors of life were no longer plaguing me. I had stopped thinking about how tired my arms were before the workout even began and I was determined to finish the workout without flinching. My attitude was that of stubborn pride and also of contentment in working towards a personal victory. It was painful and unpleasant, but I was able to get through it because I refused to let negative self-talk overwhelm me.

As my coach continued encouraging me to hit harder and with more determination until the end of the three-minute round, I clenched my teeth but felt a grimace-like smile pressing into my blistering red cheeks. At that moment, I felt strong and powerful. I was doing something my former anorexic self never imagined would have been possible. I was doing it, sweating through it, and becoming the victor of my own will.

At the conclusion of the final round, my coach fist pumped me and gave me a gentle right jab to the shoulder. "You did it, kid! With the right attitude, you can do anything!" He was right. With the right attitude and a resolute spirit, you can achieve more than you ever conceive to be possible. And by possible, I do not just mean within the realm of what I think is possible. I would like to say I think much is possible on my own, but that is not true. Yet, what is possible in God and through God is unimaginable. For through Him, all things are possible. How often do you favor that frame of mind? How often when you are grappling with something difficult or seemingly unfeasible, do you think to yourself, "No problem! I've got this! With God, I can do this! With God, this is possible!"

Perhaps you crave that "anything is possible" mindset or you just want to throw that perfect one-two punch. Or maybe, you simply want to get to the gym or wake up with the right mindset or energy to take on the day. Whatever the challenge or whatever the adversity you may be facing, you have the power to shift your mindset and to embody an attitude that believes the impossible is possible and holds steadfast to the good that can be found in all things.

Take that ready stance and be prepared to dodge the negative influences that stifle your happiness and your success. Knockout the critical thoughts that clutter your mind and stand in your way. Strikeout into the world with fearless assurance that whatever the outcome of the present moment, you will endure and you will overcome.

In your relationships with one another, have the same mindset as Christ Jesus: Who, being in very nature God, did not consider equality with God something to be used to his own advantage; rather, he made himself nothing by taking the very nature of a servant, being made in human likeness. And being found in appearance as a man, he humbled himself by becoming obedient to death — even death on a cross! (Philippians 2:5-8)

TRAIN. CONNECT. PRAY.

How will you **train** for Christ and His Kingdom today?
How will you **connect** with others today?
How will you **pray** today?

DEVOTIONAL INQUIRY:

1. **Train:** What resonated with you from this section about "Attitude and Adversity?"

   _____

   _____

   _____

2. **Connect:** How does this message connect to adversity you are currently facing in your life? How does your attitude shape your relationships, decisions, and spiritual ministry?

   _____

   _____

   _____

3. **Pray:** How will you pray today? What is the conversation you need to be having with God?

   _____

   _____

   _____

DATE: _____

GRACE IN RESILIENCE SCALE (1-10): _____

OUTLINE your action plan for _prayer, connection, and training_ in relation to "Attitude & Adversity."

   _____

   _____

   _____

Devotional Prayer

Heavenly Father,

Thank you for making me as I am! Thank you for giving me a joyful spirit and willing heart to serve others in a way that brings honor to you. I know I fall short and often compare myself to others. Help me to see you more clearly and to find confidence in both success and failure. When adversity comes my way, allow me to grow through the experience rather than to act as a victim of uncontrollable circumstance.

Lord God, help me to pursue you with endurance of mind and strength of spirit. I know you made me perfectly as I am and what I contribute to this world has meaning. I promise to shift my attitude towards healthy, positive ideas and to rid myself of the negative thoughts that filter into my mind and breed insecurity and self-doubt.

God, I am ready to take on the mission field for you! I am ready to knock out all critical or self-defeating thoughts that keep me from being close to you and ministering to the needs of others. I am prepared to be fearless in you, through you, and for you. I am your child and I am loved. And that is more than enough for me.

In your holy name I pray.

Amen.

WEEK 4

Restlessness & Reward

What do we gain from being restless?

I have always been wired to want to do more, but this mindset only serves to devalue what I am currently doing. Think about the simple paradox of wanting and doing. If I am always wanting more, it must mean that what I have does not satisfy me or lacks value in my life. Concurrently, if I am obsessively feeling the need to do more, then does that mean that what I am presently doing is lacking merit or meaning? Am I just being ungrateful in wanting more and doing more at the expense of enjoying the value in what I have?

When we continually strive for more or want to do or be better, there comes a sense of restlessness. When the constancy of movement in our lives stops, we may panic, wanting to 'do.' Then we work more frantically to fill the void spaces of time. The more unpreoccupied time we have, the more fear or worry crowd in, and the more we sense lack or imperfection. This is the cycle of "doing," but not necessarily a cycle of truly *bettering* ourselves.

A friend of mine was in postpartum. She had two children but posited that she could not wait for maternity leave to be over. She hated having too much downtime and all she wanted was return to work. Initially, I responded, reminding her of the precious gift of time she had to invest in her children. She quickly retorted that she was past the point of being bored and needed more activity. It made me wonder if we have not gotten to a place in our lives and in our culture where we are physically and emotionally unable to grasp the concept of time unless we see it moving. What is a minute? What is an hour? What is a day? What is our obsession with controlling these constructs? They are merely the simple frames through which we quantify time. But we often do not see them as such. If we are unable to enjoy downtime with a friend, a child, or a loved one, what is the underlying sense of urgency that needs to be remedied in order for us to feel fulfilled?

The dangerous mindset we often possess is that if we do more now, goodwill will come later. If I achieve all I can at this very moment, I will be satisfied with the reward that is to come. This logic is not completely flawed. We do have to work hard for what we seek to accomplish, but the thesis is not completely verifiable either. If we remain restless and drive ourselves to a detrimental state of being, will we ever enjoy the reward of our toil when it comes? Will we even realize that it is there for us? Will we, in our busyness, miss it?

Perhaps the woman in the anecdote above had worked so hard up in her life that God was providing her with a period of rest to see, experience and love her children. However, she was so caught up in the restlessness of doing, being pregnant, working full-time and becoming a mother. When the reward of freedom finally came, she shunned it away instead of seeing its value and embracing it as a gift being presented to her.

Examining a Zen perspective on this idea of "doing," Zen philosophers and practitioners hold the ideal that wanting too much and doing too much is actually a very selfish mode of being. They go so far as to label this modus operandi as being greedy. That seems to evaluate "doing" with a negative connotation, but perhaps there is something to this perspective. When we do too much and try to control time, we are often weighed down by burden and anxiety. The more we do, the less time we feel we have. Actually, we still have the same amount of time we did originally. Was the mother loathing maternity leave being greedy in wanting to fill her time with other things than what she deemed to be the mundane task of nurturing her children?

Selfishness and restlessness are two precarious attributes. Each can lead to detrimental actions or personal failure and together, they can lead to destruction.

In a similar fashion, one of the concluding chapters from my memoir, *Tatsimou, Hold On* (Adelaide Books, 2018), expresses the idea of wanting too much and doing too much. Instead of feeling satisfied, the feelings that overwhelmed me were only those of being lost and lonely in the midst of compulsive doing.

The corresponding excerpt reads as follows:

I graduated from college wearing more honor society cords than anyone else in my graduating class. Alas, I looked like Harry Potter! I had maintained a low weight while still indulging in desserts each day, and that made me feel empowered. I was an athlete with a record and a student with proven success. I was the highest-grossing marketing tool for the school. I was it. I had a job lined up if I chose to follow-through with that venture, and the prospect of graduate school awaited me as well. I thought I had it all, but in reality, I had nothing that makes life worth living. Authentic friendships remained sparse, I was not in a loving, doting, gushing relationship on course for marriage, like many of my peers, and I did not know what I wanted out of life. I had pleased and surpassed the Dean's mandated school rules and script for success. What more could I want to do? I was no longer anorexic in the physicality of having 'loss of appetite.' Rather, I was hungrier than ever before to achieve, to be, to do, more and more and more. Nothing would satisfy. As I walked across that stage, a Summa Cum Laude graduate, I was proud of myself, but numb to the moment and numb to all I had achieved. I smiled next to the President of the College with my parents standing on either side of me. I have that photograph of me in my decorated robe standing next to my weary, but pleased parents, framed with my gold, "Summa Cum Laude" tassel and it sits next to my shiny diploma exhaling achievement and success when others walk by. But when I see that slivered image in time, I count the honor society cords and see the hollow loneliness in my eyes that says, "Andrea, you did not get a 4.0. Try harder next time." The past can be a most cruel mistress. And its tentacles only widen their reach in time.

Evidently, I was not satisfied at the time of my graduation and in my compulsion to do more and be better. I was not able to discern why I was so unhappy. I was restless in every way despite the fact that I had received the reward I had wanted. It was the reward that I had told myself that I needed to attain - and I reached my goal. I should have felt fulfilled, but I was not content and I was not happy. *What was going on?* Considering this happenstance from a biblical perspective. I do not think greed would be the descriptor I would apply to these restless wants and desires, even though in a way, I was selfishly greedy. Rather, I would question whether or not I was trusting God with the time he had given me. Am I trusting God with these wants and desires? Am I allowing Him to take the lead?

We have to trust God in the rest periods of our life and know that what we set into motion will bear fruit in His time and in His way. The wheels are moving and our work has not been lost, not if we are doing the work that God wants us to do. We will be well aware of the reward when it comes our way; it will be a reward that ultimately brings glory to His heavenly Kingdom.

So, to answer the opening question about what we gain from being restless, I believe the answer is that we do not gain anything or at least not anything of intrinsic value. And unless we are working toward the thing God has called us to, we will not appreciate the reward of our toil or recognize it when it finally comes our way.

- *Trust* God in the time that he has given you.

- *Pray* that He will guide you during times when you become restless.

- *Remember* that what you are doing right now may not be what you should be doing if you are carefully listening to God's instruction.

- *Fill your time wisely* and seek out the reward that only comes from serving His kingdom, loving His world, and giving up self for others.

Therefore, my dear brothers and sisters, stand firm. Let nothing move you. Always give yourselves fully to the work of the Lord, because you know that your labor in the Lord is not in vain (1 Corinthians 15:58).

TRAIN. CONNECT. PRAY.

How will you **train** for Christ and His Kingdom today?
How will you **connect** with others today?
How will you **pray** today?

DEVOTIONAL INQUIRY:

1. **Train:** What resonated with you from this section about "Restlessness and Reward?"

_____

_____

_____

2. **Connect:** How does this message connect to your life and assessment of time? Do you think, based on the Zen definition, you are being greedy with the notion of "doing" in your life right now?

_____

_____

_____

3. **Pray:** How will you pray today? What is the conversation you need to be having with God?

_____

_____

_____

DATE: _____

GRACE IN RESILIENCE SCALE (1-10): _____

OUTLINE your action plan for *prayer, connection, and training* in relation to "Attitude & Adversity."

_____

_____

_____

Devotional Prayer

Heavenly Father,

When I am restless, help me find rest in you. When am I comparing myself to others, help me look to you. When the skein of being leaves me anxious, remind me that I am unconditionally loved. Father, forgive me for all of the ways I have selfishly served my own needs rather than those of others. Forgive me for not being satisfied by the beauty of this life you have gifted me. Forgive me for not being wholly contented in you.

Lord God, help me to seek you first and see self second. Help me to listen to your leading for my life. I know anxiety may still find a way to plague and distract me as I continue to navigate through this life, but I will do my best to not allow it to consume me. Help me to see and be present in the here and now. Thank you for the abundance of love you have placed in my life. I will do a better job to responsibly honor it, to cherish it, and to nurture it.

And finally, thank you for the sacrifice you made for me so that I may experience the greatest of all rewards, which is life eternal in you!

In your holy name, I pray.

Amen.

Faithfully Resilient

The trait of resilience is not hard to find in the Bible. From Moses to Joseph, Esther to Job, and a host of other Biblical characters, suffering or condemnation for belief in God is a continual norm of life. Moses had to endure slavery, fear, and the burden of guilt, but he eventually found himself in a position of great leadership and power. After meeting an angel from God in a burning bush, Moses led the Israelites away from Egypt following the distribution of plagues brought upon the country as directed by God. He then went on to part the Red Sea, receive the 10 Commandments, and lead the Israelites to final freedom.

Joseph, on the other hand, was betrayed by his brothers and sold as a slave into Egypt before he met redemption through interpreting dreams. Esther was forced to conceal her Jewish identity, but as Queen, she bravely devised a heroic plan that would boldly ensure that her people be spared from Haman and protected by a formal decree as he had plotted to kill all the Jews for money.

Similarly, Job was a man of wealth and good character but was tempted by Satan beyond the point of normal exasperation. God allowed Satan to torment Job with a curse upon his life and family as a means to prove Job's faithfulness. After a season, the upbraiding almost overwhelmed Job, and he became resentful and impatient in waiting for God's deliverance. He lamented the injustice he witnessed as he saw that God allowed wicked people to prosper while he and countless other innocent people suffered. He wanted to confront God, but he found the resilience necessary to act upon his faith and continue pursuing wisdom by waiting on God and standing firm against evil.

Perhaps you can relate to Moses, Joseph, Esther or Job? Your struggles may differ from theirs, but your tenacity must remain resolute. What truly matters is not the severity or circumstance of the trial, but rather the faith and resolve that these characters exhibit in the face of struggle and hardship. Moses, Joseph, Esther, and Job all stayed loyal to God's will and sovereignty, and as such, they were victorious after miserable failure or unpredictable setbacks.

As you navigate through the next four weeks of your life utilizing this devotional, examine how you can work to stay faithful during the seasons of life that test your resilience. Bear in mind that developing resilience is not easy and maintaining faith through challenges can be nothing short of tumultuous. Yet, being faithful in all things will bring restoration from the deep reserve of strength you have resting within you because of God's great love for you.

Remember, to be resilient, you first have to trust in the grip of grace that God has on your life. He has given you the gift of life for a reason and wants you to continually act as His servant, regardless of unexpected misfortune. We do not know the story that God has scripted for our lives. We can neither control it or second-guess it. What we can control is how we respond - whether we rise or fall; succeed or fail. Ultimately, we are resilient because we have faith! That is the promise of God working in us and through us! That is the shield He has extended to protect us. This faithful resilience is the reality of being a child of Christ.

Hebrews 12:1-3 counsels:

Therefore, since we are surrounded by such a great cloud of witnesses, let us throw off everything that hinders and the sin that so easily entangles. And let us run with perseverance the race marked out for us, fixing our eyes on Jesus, the pioneer and perfecter of faith. For the joy set before him he endured the cross, scorning its shame, and sat down at the right hand of the throne of God. Consider him who endured such opposition from sinners, so that you will not grow weary and lose heart.

Grace & Grit

What does it look like to practice
GRACE while cultivating GRIT?

I grew up reciting the mantra, "Saying grace is easy, practicing grace is not." The ideation of this mantra is that saying 'grace' or saying a prayer can be an easy thing to do. It may not be the most natural thing to do, but giving thanks and talking to God is not usually a difficult task even for those with little faith. However, the act of practicing grace, especially towards other people is often a difficult thing to do.

Grace can be defined as the unmerited favor of God in our lives. Grace is designed to teach us how to love and how to live. When we give grace to another person, we are actively forgiving and understanding. We are not harboring grudges or expecting apologies. We are not acting out of tolerance, but we are acting out of the example of the unconditional love we know from Christ. A simple way to remember this is to know that grace is freely given, while faith is developed through living as Christ desires and growing our relationship with Him.

When God grants us grace, He is telling us that He indeed sees our sin, but the death, the sacrifice of Christ on the cross, has covered our sin. Knowing God's grace, you should not ignore your sin or try to deal with it on your own. Because you have Christ, you have the means of grace to be set free from your sin, out of confession of sin and repentance. God allows us to rest in His humble forgiveness and when He does this, He gives us the opportunity to change through living by His example. God loves us far too much to let us be absorbed, trapped in our own sins. As a matter of fact, He loves us so much He is willing to discipline us and give us joy instead of allowing us to live in despair. His love makes grace a powerful gift to offer others. In living by His word and example, we can demonstrate grace as a sincere act of His righteousness pouring forth into our lives.

Giving grace to others as well as embracing grace for ourselves means seeing one another as new creations in Christ. We are blessed to have the opportunity to learn to risk everything for the grace He provides. His grace gives us the capacity to serve, to cherish, and to honor one another. It teaches us to give ourselves to love and to serve others because we accept that they too are worthy of Christ's unconditional love. When we see others in this way, we are acting in a redemptive manner, accepting Christ-like responsibility toward others on account of our own salvation. Galatians 6:1-2 says the following about grace:

> Brothers, if anyone is caught in any transgression, you who are spiritual should restore him in a spirit of gentleness. Keep watch on yourself, lest you too be tempted. Bear one another's burdens, and so fulfill the law of Christ.

In this passage, we learn the way of grace and as followers of Christ, we are to act firmly upon that grace. It is one way we can show Christ's love for others and act in accordance with His will.

Nevertheless, no matter how compelling and humbling grace can be, it does not mean that we will be immune to fear, and it does not mean we will not need grit both to give and receive grace. Think about grit for a moment. It can be described as courage, resolve, strength in character, or the willingness to press on despite failures or setbacks. Grit is unspoiled resilience. Grit is indefatigable. Grit, in countless studies, is the sole factor linked with the highest rates of success. Simply stated, we need to have grit in our lives. And we also need to give grace. Life can be a tough road. We will sin, fall short, and feel crippled by the weight of the world. *Grace tells us it is okay to acknowledge those things; while grit gives us the fortitude to get up and get moving again.*

When I think of grit, I think back to the competitive sports I played while growing up and throughout my college years. There were many times when I would find myself frustrated, tired, or dismayed by my performance during a meet or a game. In my despair, I would have to remind myself that the game was not yet finished and my rivals wanted to win as much or more than me. In many of those difficult competitive situations, my coaches told me to toughen up, to get back out there, to get out of my head and to refuse to back down no matter how discouraged I might have felt. Those were the moments when I clenched my teeth, said a prayer, put my game-face on, ran back onto the tennis court or dove into the cold water of a competition pool and swam until my shoulders felt numb, and I could no longer peripherally see the swimmer in the lane next to me.

On occasion, I lost a tennis match in a tie-breaker set. Or, another swimmer caught up with me at the end of the race, in a vainglorious moment of victory. But in those times of loss, my disappointed coaches did not reprimand me. Instead, they displayed grace in the face of my failure and motivated me in a way designed to fill me up with the grit I needed to carry on and train for the next competition. On account of their grace, I never once quit a team in my life, and on account of the grit I accrued under their counsel, I had the needed impetus to become stronger and to race harder and smarter. I became a better athlete because I was given grace in times of loss, but I became a great athlete because that grace provided me the room to grow and grit gave me the will to succeed.

Ponder that image of grace and grit and compare it to how you perceive its presence in your daily life. Perhaps it relates to a situation with a colleague at work or maybe with a child or a sibling. Consider times where you either had to give grace to someone who did you wrong or you received grace from someone when you fell into sinful ways. In both of these situations of giving or receiving grace, did you merely walk away after grace was given or received as though nothing had happened? Did you actively practice grit in order to right the wrong or help another individual find clarity to change their path or course of action? My assumption is that you embraced the last choice. With grace given from God, the expectation is that such a gift of grace also comes the freedom of opportunity to make changes in our personal actions and activities; changes that more clearly reflect the higher aim in life to which we are called.

While I am no longer competing in sports as I was during college, I am still competing in recreational races including triathlons, marathons, and cycling events. I am also actively working as a fitness trainer and consciously trying to balance my efforts in life, between embodying the necessary element of grace and the needed resilience of grit. Here is one example of conscientiously living by grace while intentionally maintaining grit:

> I was approached one morning after teaching a few high cardio, high strength fitness classes by a couple of the women who were in attendance. They were regulars at my classes and they were both twice my age. I have no shame in admitting, they were also twice as fit. Their finesse with social media was also impressive. They challenged me, as they also challenge ten women per day, to post a selfie on a personal social media platform that directly relates to personal gratitude. The idea is to appreciate your authentic self. In an effort to demonstrate compassion towards them and to practice grace myself, I accepted their challenge. I took a sweaty selfie in the studio in which I was working and posted it to two social media platforms. Here's what I wrote to accompany the picture.

> "No makeup. Frizzy hair. Three classes into my day, and it's only 10 AM. My legs are tired; my arms are sore; my throat is scratchy from using my voice so much. I have weird swelling in several different parts of my body. I often have overuse injuries. My head is in a heightened mode of focus for clients. My feet are still tapping eight-count bars to a beat at 145 BPM and I'm already reviewing names in my head of the next set of exercises and skill patterns. But I'm feeling so thankful. And even on the worst days, this work still unveils my smile."

I continued my reflection. The second part of my post was more about gratitude for the gift of healing and the gift of movement.

> "I am thankful for physical and psychological energy and a body that moves. A body, once stunned by self-injury, that still rallies daily and tries a little harder. I am thankful for the people who put their health first and care for their bodies. I am happy they choose me week after week as their leader: I get to motivate, test, and encourage. I am thankful for strength and healing. I may not be as thin as I once was,

but I can run, jump, swim, bike and smile. I can help others help themselves and in-between I get to share my journey towards Christ and for that, I am most grateful."

Underneath the layers, who are you as your authentic self? Where do you practice grace and how do you balance it with having grit?

Define "Grit:"

Write about how it is one of the most needed character traits to be successful long term in life. Find specific references for this and talk about it with people whom you work with or care for.

_____

_____

_____

Query "Grit:"

If we have grit or we develop it, can we still find means to demonstrate grace towards others and grace towards ourselves in our lives? Remember: *We need grit for the challenges of this life, but we need grace because we are fallen sinners seeking eternal life in His Kingdom. You cannot have one without the other.*

_____

_____

_____

For it is by grace you have been saved, through faith – and this is not from yourselves, it is the gift of God – not by works, so that no one can boast. For we are God's handiwork, created in Christ Jesus to do good works, which God prepared in advance for us to do (Ephesians 2:8-10).

TRAIN. CONNECT. PRAY.

How will you **train** for Christ and His Kingdom today?
How will you **connect** with others today?
How will you **pray** today?

DEVOTIONAL INQUIRY:

1. **Train:** What resonated with you from this section about "Grace and Grit?"

_____

_____

_____

2. **Connect:** How do you practice grace in your life? What connections can you make to situations where you needed to have *both* grace and grit?

_____

_____

_____

3. **Pray:** How will you pray today? What is the conversation you need to be having with God?

_____

_____

_____

DATE: _____

GRACE IN RESILIENCE SCALE (1-10): _____

OUTLINE your action plan for *prayer, connection, and training* in relation to "Grace & Grit."

_____

_____

_____

Devotional Prayer

Heavenly Father,

Your grace abounds! Your love astounds! Thank you for the grace you have given me in my life. Thank you for loving me as I am. Lord God, I know I make mistakes, but your grace is enough for me and it always will be. Please help me to practice having grace on others and to love them as they are and where they are. I pray for your guiding hand to show me the way of such gallant grace. Let me act in accordance with your example.

Lord God, I am determined to remain strong in you and to develop grit for the trials of this life. Remove all self-defeating thoughts that keep me from accepting your grace and help me to learn how to be bold in my faith, to trust in your mercy, and to plant, cultivate, and nurture the seeds of grit. I am nothing without you and your grace. But with the right amount of grit, I can certainly fight to sustain the joy that comes from the grace you provide.

In your holy name I pray.

Amen.

Challenge & Courage

Do you pray for challenges equal to your strength OR for strength equal to your challenges?

Surrender to Christ. I remember the first time I heard someone in my Bible study repeat that powerful phrase when I was wrestling with the decision to pursue a path for my life entirely different than what I originally thought I was 'supposed to do' for a living. I was truly confounded by the statement. "Surrender yourself to Christ and watch Him work in your life," my friend insisted. What the heck did that mean? If I was to surrender to Christ that would mean relinquishing control. My planning, obsessive-compulsive personality was terrified by that reality. How could I give up my drive and ambition? Or did I have to? Was I to work in tandem with God or was I to step back and trust His leadership? I prayed continually about this conundrum and my struggle to let go. I preferred being a leader. I wanted to have control of what was to come on the next horizon. I wanted to assume responsibility for putting the pieces in place for my success. I still struggle with this internal battle of stepping out on my own terms versus looking up and trusting His.

However, as I intentionally prayed for God's guidance in my life and anxieties slowly morphed into trusting Him, things in my life began to change. My spirit was being renewed and I was unaware of all the ways it affected me. Colleagues at work noticed an immediate change. Clients I worked with at the gym said they saw a new spark in my energy. I was writing poetry again and I was leaning into Christ and pouring over His words. By the way, if you need the best manual and self-help book for living, there's this amazing best-seller called The Bible. It just might astound you.

Keep reading and digging deeper. I promise you will not be disappointed. I promise God already figured things out for us!

As this renewal was occurring within me, I was told by others that I was radiating a new light. How powerful is that!? I would respond with a smile or a simple, "Thank you," because I knew the change in me was not because of me, but rather because of God's love living within me. Some of my selfish behaviors began to fade and my OCD-behaviors became more limited to controlling parts of my life that did not pull me away from God. Being orderly and clean is a good thing – a Biblical principle - so long as it does not become an idol. We can make idols out of "habits" or "goals," putting them above Christ. That took me some time to learn. Yet, as I continued surrendering to Christ, I became not only strong in His spirit of love but strong in my will to serve Him and to work towards improving the lives of others.

Day by day, as I toiled in a job I disliked, God began to reveal the creative pieces of me that He had fashioned and I gradually felt more and more comfortable embracing them. I journaled more frequently, wrote poems or short stories at night, and after nearly ten years of giving up on the dream of being a writer or a professional creative, I took up the torch again and set out to finish my first full-length book, apply to graduate school for an MFA in Writing, and seek out agents and publishers to represent my work.

At this point in time, I had completed about 5,000 words for a book I wanted to pursue. I needed at least 30,000-50,000 words comprising a polished manuscript to even begin entertaining the idea of developing query letters or completing book proposals. Not to mention, I also needed a solid idea to carry the story I wanted to tell and a creative way to present it. Progress was slow and I was nowhere near the track on which I needed to be proceeding to publish a book.

The first website I ever developed was a blog titled, "The Weekly Pulse." I spent a tremendous amount of time writing posts for my regular five-to-ten readers. Mind you, this was in the early 2000s and just having a blog platform was a trendy sort of accomplishment. The purpose of my blog was to explore the defining decade for young adults, their 20s, and to answer questions about navigating the seemingly endless questions and concerns that accompany that phase of life. Within my weekly posts, I wrote about everything from relationships to job opportunities, from queries about what God to what I wanted in my future. As I wrangled with life in this time period, I also began writing poetry, asking questions about finding discernment in life. The 20s are a challenging, defining period of life that often dictate the direction of the subsequent three to five decades of life. That is daunting in and of itself. Without having Christ as my anchor, I have no idea how things would have turned out for me, most especially during that period of my life.

While my fun and funky blog site dwindled after a few years, I remained interested in exploring topics about the big questions, challenges, and "what ifs" of life. Thus, I used those driving questions to catapult my then infantile book project to its next stage. At the time, I was concurrently becoming more involved in health and wellness, which also shaped my revised worldview and relationship with my body. I began asking questions revolving not around self, or what I personally wanted to do with my life, but questions about what God wanted for my life. It was an important mindset shift and allowed me to approach my life from a completely different lens. I still did not have the perfect frame for my book, but I knew if I honestly pursued developing a closer relationship with Christ, the message of chasing Him in all things and at all times, would eventually come through in a way that would resonate with others.

Entering my third year of a teaching job, I was successful, but in doing what I did not necessarily want to do. I continued to work on my book. I had found the conceptual frame for the book through the metaphor of my passion for fitness. The pieces were finally coming together. When I managed to work my way through several drafting and editing stages, I completed one final revision, polishing off the work. I then spent a few months searching for agents, publishers, and fully engaging in the exhaustive manuscript submission process. I was eager and confident, and yet, my book was rejected 17 times. No agent offered to work with me. The rejection letters were harsh. I was defeated. I promptly walked away from the manuscript and vowed never to look at it again.

God, on the other hand, had alternative plans. Three weeks after I had set my work aside, I was out for a run, when a random, new idea for the book struck me. I tried to talk myself out of it, but for some reason, even amidst a stream of rejection letters, the project was still alive, like a persistent itch, it would not go away. It was unfinished. The feedback I had received said that the manuscript lacked finality. On that 90-degree afternoon, while feeling washed away in a puddle of my own sweat, I brainstormed an innovative way to re-work the story and organize my message. What I stumbled upon was a functional way to make my book more appealing. When I returned home from my run, I skipped a shower and frantically tore up the original manuscript I had submitted and then pieced it back together, as one would do with a puzzle. Fraught with variegated emotions, I again realized, nothing was working. The genius idea I thought I had was not so genius after all. The story was in better working order than in its previous form, but it still needed a great deal of new writing, perhaps, a complete re-write. I did not have the energy for that challenge. I was at my breaking point.

A friend mentioned self-publishing to me as an option for my book, but I did not have enough disposable income to afford that risk. My pride and dignity of wanting to be a writer my entire life did not want to succumb to paying someone else to publish my work. It felt like cheating. But the system is tough and breaking into the circle of successful, published authors is difficult. I certainly understand the desires of people who self-publish. At that point, I wanted to give up on my writing dreams altogether. Who would be interested in my book? I felt like the devil was perched on my shoulder telling me that my words had no value; that I had no contribution to make in this modern, contemporary culture. But maybe the words that run counter to the culture are actually the ones we most need to hear. My story had evolved into the genre of Christian nonfiction, but it seemed flat. I knew the message I wanted to share, but I needed to engage and attract an audience. Frustrated, I sent my manuscript back to the file from whence it came and I stopped praying about it or wondering if I would ever see it published. I shifted my focus back to the daily grind the work I hated in order to distract my mind.

A month later I was out again running – my time away from technology, work, and people. In such moments, I think the clearest. I felt like God was saying to write 'me.' Write your story to tell these truths. I distinctly remember furrowing my brow, looking to the sky, like "*why*"? Who would want to read about me? How can I help someone else? What is worthwhile about me or my experiences? It was as though God was exasperated by my sarcastic questioning. Suddenly, my head swarmed with story after story from my personal life that would be fitting to the message and truths I wanted to share through my book. I was so overwhelmed that I had to stop running. I walked to my car, pulled out my journal, and feverishly made a log of all of the stories that I now wanted to tell. I felt a strong creative rush and surge of new energy. I was internally struggling, but God had made it clear to me that He did not want me to give up on the project. There was a reason I had to write this book and get it published, but that reason would not be unveiled until long after the completed book made its debut into the world.

Nevertheless, responsive to God's guidance, the following weekend I infused my weary manuscript with personal anecdotes and used the frame of endurance training as a motif to weave the story together. I told stories in a fiction-writing format and I used my observational skills to pull out details from the stories that would impress upon my readers the importance of the messages I was led to share. I was breathing life back into my book and I knew it. Maybe, just maybe, this book would have a second chance at making it into the world.

As the book developed and took on a new shape, I began to work on revised query letters and I strengthened my personal platform to craft a distinctive foundation for my formal book proposal. With many prayers, I selected three more publishers for my proposal hoping to receive a positive response. Surprised, but thankful, two out of the three agreed to read the full manuscript which I sent with great expedience. I was excited at the possibility of seeing my work in print. A couple of weeks later, one of the publishers wrote back saying they were interested in publishing my book. Wait, what? Someone was interested in publishing my message? My words? I was ecstatic when I finally received that albeit modest offer for my book. I had no agent, but that also meant, no fees. I was accepted for publication on the sheer merit of my work and it was beyond gratifying. I felt validated and was eager to begin the publishing process.

I was absolutely giddy, but unfortunately, life does not always go our way. Four months later, the work on my book came to an immediate halt. The entire contract tanked. The publisher went out of business, suspended all projects, and took my aspiring hopes as a writer along with them. I was soon empty of hope and hard-pressed to find even an ounce of courage remaining within me. Challenge and courage. That's the Christian life, right? Perhaps I had misread God's will. Maybe it was not meant to be. Maybe something was missing. May this was not my time. I dove back into my daily labors and again tried my best, but I could not forget about the book. I had labored over the project and invested so much love. I had been so close to completing the project. Did I really have to give up? Who was telling me to do so? I prayed with my heart in surrender to Christ and I researched publishers and agents one last time. I made some small tweaks to my manuscript and bolstered my personal portfolio. One last shot. I would give it one last shot, and then if nothing came through, I would move onto a new project or just table the fallacy that I would ever become a legitimate author.

I selected one more publisher. The publisher was listed as one of the top five Christian publishers and they were in a phase of accepting unsolicited manuscripts. I gave my submission my very best effort from a fresh cover letter to a persuasive, polished book proposal. I heard back from them in less than two weeks and they requested to view my entire manuscript. I sent it out but did not expect any response or further contact from them. I presumed rejection as that was becoming a conditioned norm for me. I was more jaded than I had been the last time around as my hopes to see my book in print were dashed after a four-month ride of anticipation.

But God has His own timing for us and for our lives. If we can accept that truth, He can show us beauty that we never would have expected. I will never forget that on the morning of December 1st, the day I was planning to submit my resignation letter at work, which would enable me to pursue graduate school full time. I opened my email and saw a formal letter from the last publisher to which I had sent my submission. In the letter, my book was praised, and the editor said their company was fully behind my message and were eager to guide me through the publication process. I stared into my computer screen and then restarted my computer to make sure the email was there and that it was indeed real. Later that same day, I received a personal call and a contract offer for *Finding the Finish Line*. I was filled with God's grace at that moment and I knew what had happened was the right thing at the right time. It was a far more reputable publisher than the previous one with which I had dealt. I was about to leave my job, so I would have more time available to devote to marketing and promoting the story I so badly wanted to share with the world.

I honestly admit, if I had not gotten that contract that morning, I might have backed out of quitting my job and pursuing my passion. I had been feeling that I was a failure as a writer. I wasn't certain I could finish and publish my book, despite the fact that I had been admitted to an elite graduate school for writing. Staying in the job and keeping the comfortable paycheck was incredibly tempting. But this was my sign, my cue from heaven. A traditional, stable publishing company with an excellent reputation wanted me to sign with them! God had not just made a path for me, He led me to it. And He willingly showed me the way once I fully placed my heart and trust in Him. My journal entry that evening began with the following statement:

God is always speaking. It is up to us to listen.

In the months that followed, I worked towards the official release of my first book and poured into graduate school studies. I experienced success with the book and I learned a great deal about publishing. I ventured into public speaking and found more avenues to pursue writing both personally and professionally.

I must admit, however, that in those few years after leaving my full-time job, I struggled financially and the stress of that burden felt onerous to me. Yet as promised, God filled my heart and my life in so many unexpected ways that might not have been available to me had I continued on the path I was positioned on. The opening question of this chapter asks, "Do you pray for challenges equal to your strength or for strength equal to your challenges?" During that early writing phase of my life, I learned how to pray for strength equal to my challenges. Money was a challenge, but it did not have to consume me. I could live with less and I could learn to delay gratification. I could learn to live life not to fill voids with things that money could provide, but rather to fill voids with God's love and abundant grace. It is amazing what He provides for us. It is disparaging that we barely take notice.

I still drive a beat-up Honda Civic and aside from getting my nails done, I am not about to entertain many frivolous expenses. I exercise at the gyms where I work in order to save on a gym membership and I eat dinner with my parents many nights during the week. I moved back home for a few years during graduate school. But what I gained from these challenges was far more than I ever anticipated. During that time, my first book was published and I began the process of writing a second one. I commenced several other writing projects, none of which have avenues to publication as of yet, but I had the time to freely write and to create. I completed my MFA in Writing, which took me out to Enders Island for my studies. It is one of the most spiritually evocative places I have ever visited and I knew each time I was there that I was exactly where God wanted me to be.

In addition, I discovered love and security in a man, now my husband, who would do anything for me – also something I never believed I would have in my life. I developed professionally as a freelance writer managing editing projects and feature writing assignments and also progressed towards certifications in my other passions: fitness, health, and wellness. I became a top trainer in my local community and as a leader in holistic living, I have been able to share the gift of movement and my love of Christ with others every single day. And perhaps the best gift of all during that time of financial woes and part-time work was that I had more time for family and friends. I was able to join new groups, serve at church, and invest in new relationships. I learned how to confidently take the opportunity to spread the Gospel and lead others in the way of Christ.

As I write this, during this particular week of my life, I will host another church-centered event wherein I will speak about *Finding the Finish Line* as well as my memoir, *Tatsimou, Hold On!*, and my debut poetry collection, *Forgotten Coffee*. None of these things would have been possible without the call God placed on my heart or my willingness to pursue that call despite setbacks and challenges. God will always provide for our wants and needs if we let Him. The journey may not be easy, but it is on that journey wherein we gain strength and grow in His love and experience His mercy.

Furthermore, I witnessed something very similar to my own struggle with a job I disliked as I recently watched my husband wrestle with career decisions and an unfavorable working environment. He was feeling trapped with no way out. It is an abrasive feeling to be in that position and it is scary to feel so uncertain of day to day responsibilities when you loathe where you are and what you are doing. I watched him pray. I watched him lean on God. I witnessed his immense courage as he got up to drive an hour and a half to work each and every day. I knew he felt the burden of wanting to provide for me and for our lives together and I saw the mental and physical toll it was taking on him. But what he did was put God out front. He trusted in the Lord and as I prayed for him, I also searched for security in the steadfast words of our church community.

At this time of frustration and confusion, as I was looking for more work and my husband was seeking work opportunities away from where he was planted, God taught us to trust in each other and to trust in God's plans for us! We were facing challenges and pressures, but what we could rely on was having courage in Christ and faith in each other as we walked closer towards him together. It was not easy. It is not supposed to be. Learning to make changes, being bigger than our fears, and having the courage not just to take the first step, but to take every single step after that first one without giving up, is hard! But we must take heart! We must hold on and we must rest in the assurance of His love. I promise he will astound us.

Our happiness does not come without challenges, but so does our faith. It takes courage to live in Christ. If I am happy having nothing if I still have Christ, then I have figured out what it is to know and to serve Him. I am now able to call myself a writer, a published author, but I would first, prefer to call myself a daughter of Christ.

Trust in the Lord with all of your heart and lean not on your own understanding; in all your ways, acknowledge Him and He will keep you paths straight (Proverbs 3:5-6).

TRAIN. CONNECT. PRAY.

How will you **train** for Christ and His Kingdom today?
How will you **connect** with others today?
How will you **pray** today?

DEVOTIONAL INQUIRY:

1. **Train:** What resonated with you from this section about "Challenge and Courage?"

_____

_____

_____

2. **Connect:** What challenges are you facing in your life? How has God provided you with courage to overcome these challenges?

_____

_____

_____

3. **Pray:** How will you pray today? What is the conversation you need to be having with God?

_____

_____

_____

DATE: _____

GRACE IN RESILIENCE SCALE (1-10): _____

OUTLINE your action plan for *prayer, connection, and training* in relation to "Challenge & Courage."

_____

_____

_____

Devotional Prayer

Heavenly Father,

Thank you for giving me the courage to stand up for you in the midst of life's chaos and disenchantment. Thank you for challenging me to remain in you and in your word even when I have doubts. I pray that I will be able to seek your glory above my personal wants and desires at all times and in all seasons of adversity.

Lord, you have shown me that your provision is far greater than I could ever imagine and the patience required for your endowment upon my life is worthwhile. Allow me to embrace life's challenges with both courage and grace. Let me actively practice my love for you so that others may witness the steadfast nature of my trust in you.

I know you will not leave me and you will not forsake me. As I wrestle with financial, emotional, or relational stressors in life, help me to lean on you and to move forward with you in the comfort of your love. When I feel weary or lack in trust, please help me look to you and know that the story of my life has already been beautifully scripted by your most masterful hand.

In your holy name I pray.

Amen.

Trial & Trust

When your faith is shaken,
how do you respond? Does hardship bring you closer to
Christ and the glory of His eternal kingdom
or does it draw you further away?

RESILIENCE IN THE LOVE OF CHRIST & FAMILY

Protective paralysis overwhelmed my body the day my Mom was first diagnosed with cancer. I was fifteen years old.

Resilience has as much to do with the body as it does the mind. We have a physical attachment to this world and the things it contains. The physical bond we have with our own bodies determines how our nerve endings perceive the world and experience life. Yet, what drives all of the physical sensations is our perception of what they are and how they feel. It is our mind that determines our reactions to these sensations and ultimately controls them. Sometimes they can be more intense than others. Often they cannot be tamed as we wish. Resilience is earned over time and through experience. If we are not resilient in our minds or able to practice mental resilience, we will not exhibit any sort of physical shrewdness within our lives. Yet through faith, hope, and deliverance, we can grow and persist.

Twelve years following my mother's very involved and traumatic breast cancer treatment, and fifteen years to the date of her initial diagnosis, something went terribly awry. Perhaps it was happening gradually, but we remained unaware, our minds sheltering us as we avoided the guilt of impending responsibility. But something horrific happened. My mother woke up one morning and the haunting scars across her chest were swollen and red. The right side of her chest was enlarged, appearing as a balloon, growing rapidly. Burdened by this new pain and discomfort, the taut skin of her scars appeared to frown as the swelling beneath her skin continued to overwhelm the barren space on her chest. With each shallow breath she took, she cringed and cried. My mother, the once all-courageous cancer survivor, was fearful.

"What's wrong, Peter? What's happening?" Mom pleaded with my father, a physician, who always wished to deny the reality of medical problems that involved those he loved and cherished.

"Honey," he responded softly. "Let's wait a few days and see what happens. Perhaps it is swelling or aggravated tissue," he said.

"But this pain, this pain," she replied. "I can't handle this pain."

As I observed their exchange, witnessed Mom's fear and encouraged Dad's embrace of her, I felt paralyzed. I felt I lacked any capacity for resilience. My mother's pain, her fear, and the discussions of the unknowns left me in a heightened state of unease.

The surgeon who had performed her double mastectomy ten years prior instructed Mom, in her new condition, to wear a sling to rest her left arm and restrict most movement through her chest and upper body for a week. The treatment was minimal and the hope was that the swelling would dissipate and the pain would lessen if the tissues were not being consistently aggravated by movement. I watched her in the days that followed, stubborn as ever, not rely on anyone but herself, whether she was doing dishes or folding laundry with one hand, with the other arm in a sling. She cooked and cleaned and made all sorts of phone calls. She was not exactly immobilizing her chest. As I witnessed her obstinacy, my thoughts wandered to my high school years and her original battle with breast cancer. The very same illness that took her mother's life seemed to be resurfacing in her as a sort of reincarnated plague.

I reminisced about the morning of her double mastectomy, my older brother was abroad studying in Guatemala, and my younger sister, in eighth grade, was at school. Dad demanded her to be near others that day. I, in obedience and with anxiety, took the day off, skipping my high school classes to be with my Dad. That very day, I witnessed the strongest man I have ever known weaken, falling to his knees in despair.

The decision at the time was unsettling. It demanded that Mom undergo a mastectomy, followed by an oophorectomy, hysterectomy, and then more chemotherapy. Yet we were confident it was the right thing to do. We were informed that the mastectomy would take place right after Christmas. At the beginning of January, my older brother left for his collegiate January term. It involved a service-learning trip to Guatemala. He was reassured by my mom that everything would go well with the surgery. She didn't want him to worry. I was amazed at how well she held it together as we said goodbye at the airport.

My mom's mother lost her battle with breast cancer in 1995 and I was not at all prepared to lose my mother. Each day, as the surgery approached, we prayed together as a family. Our nerves were mounting, sleepless nights endured, and fear, overcome with worry, was our chief burden. Mom worked to ready herself for the surgery. Dad, the doctor who knew too much about her exact type of breast cancer, survival rates, complications with surgery, etc., kept relatively quiet. Still, he did not stop encouraging, loving, and praying for Mom.

January 10th, 2008 was surgery day for Mom, and the day when the culmination of fear, anxiety, and stress came to a climax. Through my father's actions and reactions during the day, I finally came to fully understand the meaning of resilience in love. Dad had considered working on the day of Mom's surgery, probably to distract himself from the reality of the situation. He has never missed a day of work in his life. On this day, all of his peers, the doctors, and nurses with whom he worked counseled him to take the day off. He needed distance from the hospital and from people, as well as the challenges of work. My Dad knew the surgeon who was performing the double mastectomy and was told he would be updated as the surgery progressed. The most important piece of information on which he was waiting was news about whether or not Mom's cancer had spread into her lymph nodes and thus, further into her body. If cancer, which was present in both breasts, had not spread, my mother would have a much better chance of survival. But if cancer had spread to the lymph nodes, we all knew what that meant, even though my Dad refused to say anything to that effect.

That morning as Mom was undergoing a lengthy, seven-hour surgery, we sat together, Dad and me, at a breakfast diner where we normally chowed down on stacks of fluffy pancakes with sugary maple syrup cascading down the sides. Dad would drink copious cups of coffee and I would complain of being stuffed. But that day, we both sat in silence and stared at an untouched stack of strawberry pancakes neatly dusted with powdered sugar accompanied by an ice cream-sized scoop of creamed, whipped butter. The pancakes were not very fluffy and the powdered sugar did not dance on the heated plate as it normally did. The syrup I poured barely slid off the pancakes. It looked more like molasses sludge than maple syrup. Dad's side-order of rubbery sausage did not sizzle. The coffee was cold, without the normal wisps of steam. Gray hairs I had never noticed before lined the crown of Dad's receding hairline – his aging seemed more aggressive, or at least to me, it was more visible. His watch battery had died and the clock face mocked us at 9:05 AM. It continued to do so for two more hours of empty stares. Untouched pancakes and a crusty, burnt piece of uneaten toast that I compulsively smothered with orange marmalade were our companions. We both hated jam, especially textured marmalade.

When the check came, we remained motionless at the table.

"Would you like a to-go box?" the waitress inquired. Neither of us responded. She walked away, not expecting any form of a tip from us. Waiting on a phone call from the hospital with an update, Dad checked his watch.

"Still 9:05, kid. Did anyone call you?" The time warp reminded us that it was too soon to know anything. I reached into my pocket and pulled out my phone. It was nearly noon. There had been no calls from the hospital or the surgeon made to my phone.

"Do you think Mom is going to be okay?" My teenage pimples and near-anorexic body feared the worst. Dad opened another little carton of marmalade and spread it onto the edges of the same sad piece of burnt toast.

"Pray. All you can do is pray," he said. I looked into his oversized coffee mug. Still no steam, but for some reason, I expected there to be some. Instead, I saw the reflection of two gaunt faces shattered by emotional anguish, suffering from most hollow devastation.

When we arrived home after our time at the diner, we walked our dogs, who also sensed our tension, and we continued to wait. Pacing back and forth in our kitchen, shaking, crying, holding hands with me and not knowing how to handle himself, Dad finally got the call he had been waiting for all day. A call he should have received by 12:00 noon, now came in the late afternoon. He picked up the phone. His face looked as though it had aged ten years in one day.

"Yes. Okay. Thank you," he said. "When will she be done?" Tears immediately began streaming down my father's face as the disjointed conversation continued. I feared the worst. I thought the dreaded news was now official. Dad hung up the phone in silence. He didn't say a word. My eyes started watering and I sat motionless on the floor near his feet waiting for him to move his lips. I wanted him to say something, anything! After taking a few wobbly steps forward, he fell to his knees in the middle of our kitchen and sobbed uncontrollably. I didn't know if the news was good or bad. I had only seen my father cry that way one other time in my life, that was when he lost his father. I couldn't help but cry when I looked at Dad; it was good to relieve all of the pent-up emotions I had experienced that day.

Through somber eyes, Dad finally looked up at me and whimpered, "The cancer has not spread. There was only a microscopic amount in the lymph nodes on the right side, but it has not spread to her body." I wept with joy as Dad kept saying, "Thank you, God, thank you, God, thank you, God! He pulled himself from the ground and with a surge of adrenaline flowing through his body, literally started jumping for joy. He bounded about the kitchen, picked me up and swung me around, smiling and repeating, "Yes! Yes! Yes! Woo!" He filled our house with shrieks of joyous, passion, and sheer, unbridled emotion.

A few fist pumps later, he ran out the front door and started doing laps around our home. He was overwhelmed by elation, relief, and the deep love and devotion he felt towards my mother. I had never seen him respond to anything in such an emotional way. I was in disbelief. I cried for my mother. I cried just watching my father and knowing how much he loved and cherished his wife. Seeing him react that day, I did not just feel love or have the experience of love – I actually came to fully understand love.

Love is not the warm, fuzzy feeling you get when your dog lies by your feet. Love is not the feeling that accompanies the simple hug from a friend at the end of a long day. Love is not pancakes in bed on your birthday. Love is resilient. Love is an indescribable emotion that transcends feeling. It is the quintessence of compassion and the utmost desire of the human spirit that connects us to others. On that cold, January day, I learned just how much my father loved my mother. I learned how much he needed, respected, admired, and cared for her. She is everything to him – a part of his world he cannot imagine being without. In the spectrum of human emotion, love is perhaps the most powerful and zealous of all. No form of cancer can destroy that love.

Folding my Dad's socks and undershirts against the counter with her right hand, her left arm in a sling, I told myself that Mom needed me to be strong for her. Though it felt as if no time had passed since I sat at that diner awaiting her sentence, actually, a lot of time had elapsed. I reflected on the changes. My pimples were gone and only faded scars remained in their place. Muscular development from my work as a fitness trainer disguised my formerly emaciated frame. A few gray hairs had begun to surface in my thick, brown hair. My brother was now married and considering having children. My sister had recently completed a doctorate in Physical Therapy. Dad was still lively, but overworked and getting older. Mom looked shorter than I remembered her in the early years and her shoulders hunched to a greater degree than when I was in high school. Her face was thinner and the coloration of her skin was duller. Life had changed, but in many ways, we had not. The fearlessness I craved was nowhere to be found. I did not want the doctor to again sentence my mother to cancer.

I felt the same childlike weakness I had known ten years before. This time, I was not a kid, but rather, an adult daughter. It was different. Mom could rely on me in ways she could have done before. Then, I felt helpless to fix anything. Out of pride, Mom tried to refuse my help with laundry or in making dinner or even walking the dog. I helped where I could and as she would allow.

Mom's condition gradually worsened and a few days later, Dad ordered me to help more. He also informed me that I would be attending an appointment with Mom at the local hospital's cancer center the following week. Baldness now appeared in the place where gray hairs had once crowned Dad's forehead. But his affirmative tone in speaking to me had not changed. It was exactly as it had been ten years prior.

"You take care of your mother. You are to be here for her. Listen. Be present. Do that for me," he cried through cracked, tired lips. He wanted me to fill in all the gaps where he felt that he fell short. He wanted me to emotionally support Mom in ways he sensed that he was inadequate. He wanted me to sacrifice my own work and obligations. His work demands, he believed, were too great to neglect. His shortcomings as a husband were to be compensated by me as her daughter. It was impossible. No matter how hard I might try, I could never replace his role as my mother's husband, a role only he could fulfill. Mom needed me, but she needed him more. That fact would never change.

The following week, I sat in the waiting room for nearly two hours as Mom was being evaluated for her chest pain and swelling. As I did, an enormous pocket formed in my own chest. I did not want to lose my mother. I did not want her sentenced by the doctors to a battle with cancer again. Flashbacks taunted me and nerves made my flutter uncomfortably. Mom and I were in the midst of planning my wedding. I needed her. There was no way she could be sick. This was *not* happening again.

When she returned to the waiting room two hours later, I was informed that the results of the testing were inconclusive. Further tests were ordered. I wanted to know what the doctors were doing during those two hours. Rather than beleaguer her with questions, I distracted her thoughts with a discussion about my latest graduate school project. Mom was always interested in my school achievements. She had been in support of education my whole life. As we drove home, we listened to instrumental Christmas music on the radio. She was quiet. It was early December and she was my Christmas present, now passenger in the seat next to me, moaning in harrowing pain.

"Honey, can you make dinner tonight?" she asked, not wanting to afflict me with the responsibility. "Can you prepare something for Dad and your sister?" I saw her struggle to relinquish control as care-taking was being surrendered to me again. Mom was hurting and even though I was capable of taking care of things, I was more than scared.

I steadied my quivering lips and cleared my throat. "I will make dinner, okay? Don't worry, Mom. Don't worry." She closed her eyes and rested until we arrived home.

It is mystifying the way our minds work in certain moments. We experience flashbacks, both at points when our lives are characterized by fast-paced movements and then, in isolation. The mornings of frozen pancakes and the hours of waiting, followed by ten years of gray-hair-producinganxiety and concern had passed. There was no mistaking that Mom and Dad had aged during that time, but the discomforting feelings about cancer and the fear of losing my mother were the same. I felt responsible for Mom's well-being, as before, and for our family. I had to make sure our family still had a Christmas. I had to step up and grow up and be the adult I had never wanted to be an innocent high school teen passively awaiting Mom's diagnosis.

Driving to work in the pre-dawn dark at 5:00 AM the next day, I was immersed in the silence of the morning. Tears multiplied in my eyes and at that moment, I wanted to go back in time. Back to the family road trips that took us to nearly all 50 states and to the young, healthy parents that I had taken for granted. I wanted to return to the endless laughter, to the dinners with grandparents, to escape to the days when there was no worry about money or bills, travel plans or whether or not Santa was real. A swarm of warmth flooded my mind. All of the moments, the life memories Mom and Dad had created for me and my siblings were almost tangible. All the time I had spent wishing to be older, wishing to grow up, I wanted to redeem. All the time I had wished for the adult life, to do all the adult things that I now seemed to despise, I wanted back. Those early years, the times with Mom, Dad, and our family together, they now seemed to be the best, the most meaningful moments of my life. They brought me to back to a virtual place of familial love and hope. I wanted it all once again. My hands trembled on the steering wheel. My tears soon dried as I focused on the classes that I was scheduled to teach that morning.

Though I could not recognize it then, in that very moment, that cold, dark Monday morning, visiting with all of those moments and memories gave me the resilience that I needed at that point in my life. That strength from our familial bond of love had such deep roots that it would not be easily supplanted. And that is what made me feel wholeness despite the hollowness of my flittering tummy, filled only with the almost frozen, day-old coffee that had lifted from my cup-holder and casually sipped. The bliss of the Christmas season was tangible, but the anxiety of the unknown was still upsetting. As we develop endurance in life, we become more aware of the cyclical nature of our feelings as we reflect upon past traumas and experiences. As our minds process current events and challenges against the backdrop of past experiences, we are provided with scaffolding to better interpret our lives and make more informed decisions. The lesson I am learning now is that I need to draw on such resources, so that I can have the emotional maturity to experience strength for the present moment.

In the paralysis I felt after I finished work that day, I remembered what a missionary friend of mine told me about life and its continual struggle between joy and grief. She said to me that we spend much of our lives balancing joy in one hand and grief in the other. The metaphor worked well for me. The joy, she explained, is to remind us of why we live. The grief is what keeps us humble. So much of life involves trial and struggle. God gives us an abundance of joy, but He doesn't promise us a life free from pain. Joy is God's blessing for our journey. We have to delicately maintain balance to temper the sadness or grief while not forgetting the joy of life's blessings. I was cradling both that Christmas, and I was prepared to give Mom some of the joy I knew she needed to balance out the hefty weight of her own personal sorrow.

The lights on the Christmas tree at my parents' home blurred each time I looked at it. It had been decorated during an evening of agony, impatient argument, and even yelling. But through my mind's eye, I only wanted to see the delightful memories of past Christmases. That is, of course, their purpose, I falsely believed. Firmly planted. Aptly welcomed and received. You can't have joy without sorrow. You can't have life without loss. In a strange way, I felt that the Christmas tree radiated the love of Christ my family needed.

Mom went for an MRI and additional testing a week later. Joy and grief were solemnly resting in equal balance when we got the test results back. Mom's diagnosis would remain unknown. She would go for surgery where her chest would be cut open, cleaned out, and examined the week before Christmas. She was a fighter and we would not let go of the hope, the love, or the memories that knitted our family together.

The fuzzy, polychrome lights on the tree gave me faith that as God had done the past, He would grant Mom resilience in mind and in body as she faced surgery and a period of renewal in healing. And that Christmas, as Mom recovered, God would once more gift our family with newfound patience, grace, and eternal understanding.

When you pass through the waters, I will be with you; and through the rivers, they shall not overwhelm you; when you walk through fire you shall not be burned, and the flame shall not consume you (Isaiah 43:2).

TRAIN. CONNECT. PRAY.

How will you **train** for Christ and His Kingdom today?
How will you **connect** with others today?
How will you **pray** today?

DEVOTIONAL INQUIRY:

1. **Train:** What resonated with you from this section about "Trial & Trust?" How does God work in your life when you face uncertainty?

_____

_____

_____

2. **Connect:** How will you connect this message or your experiences to serve those around you? Does fear prevent you from trusting in God's plan and provision for your life?

_____

_____

_____

3. **Pray:** How will you pray today? What is the conversation you need to be having with God? (I have included my personal devotional reflection and prayer for this section below.)

_____

_____

_____

DATE: _____

GRACE IN RESILIENCE SCALE (1-10): _____

OUTLINE your action plan for _prayer, connection,_ and _training_ in relation to "Trial & Trust."

_____

_____

_____

Devotional Reflection & Prayer

I think that in the end, all we truly want is assurance and strength. We want to be able to trust and believe in something greater than ourselves because this life is too hard to tackle on our own. No matter how many vices we indulge in to fill the void - work, activities, hobbies, addictions - there remains a longing and there remains a sadness.

Being fearless in our walk with Christ means achieving fulfillment in him. It means resting in him. It means stopping the compulsion of doing and embracing the grace of resting. Being fearless in Christ means that we trust in him without any hint of doubt.

The evening before my mom went in for her surgery over ten years post-mastectomy, I was uneasy, but felt resilience and hope would only come in full trust and reliance upon Christ. So, I prayed the following prayer again and again until peace whelmed my heart and assurance grasped hold of my being.

Heavenly Father,

Please bless and protect Mom. Please give her a sense of inner peace and calm about her being. Overwhelm her with your strength and help her to value your endless blessings upon her life. Please guide the surgeon's hands and assist him in his work. Lord, please take care of my family as we strive to be strong for Mom. Bring rest to my father and sister. Bring renewed happiness to Mom. Lord God, I ask that you bring patience, grace, and forgiveness into our lives. Heavenly Father, I thank you and I praise you. Thank you for this life, for your love, for your abounding spirit that resides within us. Give us smiles and grateful hearts. Give us love and inner peace.

In your most holy name, I pray.

Amen.

Disappointment & Distraction

What does it mean to be fiddle-footed?

If someone calls you "fiddle-footed," it means they are referring to you as a reckless wanderer. In a similar fashion, you might also be labeled as "lost" or "without direction." For all intents and purposes, I prefer "fiddle-footed." After all, it is far more fun to say! While wandering aimlessly now and then might be okay, wandering recklessly and without good intentions or a strong sense of purpose is not how God calls us to act. He does not want us to be fiddle-footed. Instead, He wants us to be sure-footed, placing our trust in His direction for our lives at all times.

We are, without question, to keep our focus on God, rather than on the many tempting distractions of this world and we are to willingly place trust in His leadership for our lives. This often feels like an uncomfortable form of trust because it is rooted in having faith in an unknown outcome. We do not know the end of the story, but we have to trust in God's plan and the beauty He has designed for our lives. Sure, on the other hand, the life of reckless wandering appears far more freeing and quixotic! It is a life without worry about what is to come. Although it may sound enticing, it is not the life God calls us to or for which he made us! He designed us with a distinct, personal purpose. If we are not paying attention to what is happening in our lives or to God's will for us, we are not acting out of love towards Him. Instead, we are acting selfishly upon our own wants, needs, and desires. We are ultimately responsible for the course of our lives. If we remain fiddle-footed, that is a choice we are consciously making. We can walk with God or walk away from Him. Choose wisely.

Scrolling through my Facebook newsfeed after a 5:00 AM fitness class, I saw photos and posts of my cyber friends as they recapped their weekends. Some had adventures to the zoo or vacationed in some breathtaking destination. Others had finished a project on their house. Some boasted about the accomplishments of their children. Others posted about some loss or hardship. The posts ran the gamut in regard to subject matter, but they all carried the same underlying message. First of all, we have a need to be seen – or why would so many people participate in sharing over social networks? And secondly, we want to feel a part of community. Social networks provide virtual community and in many ways, they are an uplift and allow us to feel connected, but it is just that – a virtual reality, and we must caution against our reliance upon it or our chosen interaction within it.

As I continued to distract myself in the throes of the lives of others, I realized that the last thing I was focused on at that moment was God. Rather than praying for those friends whose posts were less than enthusiastic, all I did was compare myself to those happy photos and to the relationships they depicted, making me envious of the cool cars and getaways for which I did not have the money. The new homes and growing families along with the fact that I did not have a hand in everything it seemed others were doing was a bright contrast to the 'nothing' it seemed that I was doing. Then I scrolled my own homepage. I had a post-race selfie of a marathon, a cookout with family, posts about my writing, pictures of the gyms at which I work and posts related to fitness and health. Suddenly I saw the contradiction of all the shiny glossy happiness I did not consciously feel on most days, but certainly didn't fail to express on Facebook.

I seemed drawn to relish in my unfulfilled wants and needs as a kind of distraction, while, at the same time, trying to make myself feel better by counting the "likes" on one of my Facebook posts. I tried to figure out why the heck I felt so disappointed. Was it the social media so good at making me feel this way? Was it because my gauge of "goodness" or "happiness" was predicated on validation from others? Was I comparing my status to others? I scrolled through two more political posts and about seven more heavily filtered selfies before I reached my "enough." I was being swallowed up by something in which I had willingly elected to participate. I logged out and deleted the Facebook app on my phone. I didn't need my screen cluttered with glossy images, rants, or even tragic news stories from everyone else's world. I needed to return from the disheartening distraction and center my heart and mind on things above, not things in the vapid cloud of virtual reality.

After taking a full week off of social media and limiting my cell-phone usage to actual phone calls, I noticed a change. As though I was an addict trying to break a habit, at first I struggled, but I also thrived. I began noticing people more. You know, those real-life everyday people that we encounter in our daily lives. I began investing more deeply in my real, rather than virtual friendships. Rather than messaging people, I offered to meet them in-person for a walk or a cup of coffee. In so doing, I made connections. I fostered relationships and developed a sense of tangible community. In my downtime, when I would normally browse social media, I took to reading through a chapter of the Bible. I chose Romans. It had appropriate guidance for the shift I needed to make in my life.

By day seven of my media diet, I felt enlightened and refreshed. I no longer needed to fill empty spaces with an unhealthy media distraction and I was no longer disappointed or overwhelmed by feelings that my life story did not match up to the stories of others. I still use social media. It is difficult to avoid. However, I have a detached or intentionally distant perspective about it and what happens in that environment. We all want to be seen and be a part of a community. Perhaps it is best to be seen as we are seen by God – as who we are and for what we are. It is time for us to allow ourselves to see others and be seen in places other than behind the security of our computer screen.

Away from endurance training, in the off-season, I sincerely enjoy boxing. Training for boxing ensures I will not be tempted towards fiddle-footed behaviors or attitudes. Not to mention, there is something rather empowering about wrapping your hands and wrists, putting on boxing gloves, and throwing punches at a partner. I have been fortunate that my boxing partner has long been my younger sister. She is strong, determined, and she pushes me past the limits of my comfort zone. I am generally frustrated by the traits she exhibits during our sessions together. I sometimes wish I could take the gloves off and literally knock her out! Okay, I am teasing. I love her with all my heart, but she sure makes me work hard. And though I may feel a tinge of belligerence during our sessions, afterward, when the soreness from the work sets in, I find myself grateful for her tenacity in pushing me to work harder and become stronger.

My sister and I often partake in classes where one person holds the mitt while the other throws the punches. We work in an alternating pattern between catching punches and throwing them. The sets are programmed on a three-minute round rotation in which we cycle back and forth through various combinations. We throw straight punches numerically called "on-two" punches, hooks called "three-four" punches, uppercuts called "five-six" punches, and then knock-out punches. Occasionally, we will incorporate some other direct punches designed to mimic specialty hits to a body part such as the infamous "liver shot." The coach directs us through different rhythmic combinations of punches and we move through each round until we reach nearly complete musculoskeletal fatigue. The aim is to hit hard and to be accurate with each subsequent punch in the sequence, which becomes more difficult as exhaustion intensifies. We are coached to stay light on our feet and to keep our guard up regardless of whether we are the one punching or the one receiving the punches. At the conclusion of the workout, we finish with a super-set of fast, aggressive, consecutive punches rotating only between jabs, hooks, and uppercuts.

Boxing is a rigorous, fast-paced sport, and it offers a stimulating recreational workout. It is imperative in boxing that you remain alert and ready throughout the sets. Unlike other workouts in which one might be able to get away with taking it easy now and then, or set one's own pace, that is not an available option when someone is throwing punches at your face. In recreational boxing, your partner sets the pace for each round and one either pays attention and keeps up, or risks getting hit in the face or another body part. In such moments, if I am not alert or holding my mitts steadily when my partner strikes, we will experience an unsuccessful round. Both partners involved can suffer from arm, wrist, or back injuries from using the improper technique. If the mitt holder is not holding a steady, firm base, and the person punching is not using good form or hitting accurately, both parties suffer.

In regard to training purposes, I find this observation to be an ironic truth. Boxing is a sport that, in the professional realm, is solely reliant on a winning individual. Competition is between two people, but there is only one winner. For my sister and I, not seeking to win or lose, we have to work together, as a pair, so we both benefit from the workout. When boxing as my sister and I do, there is a strong element of trust and teamwork within our working partnership. Being lax when hitting or catching blows is simply is not an option. I can attest to this. Unfortunately, I have gotten injured in the position of mitt holder. Usually, this happens when I am not alert or not focused on the immediacy of the punches I am to be catching. It also occurs when I allow myself to get caught up with life stressors that are upsetting me outside of the ring. In order to filter such things out, we must be intentional about our presence in the moment and the task in front of us. Having that filter enables us to then return to those outside stressors at another time with a renewed lens of assurance and purpose. After all, if was in the midst of an actual sparring match and I was not alert or did not fully 'show-up,' I would be out within the first round.

Life sometimes works this way, too. If we are not alert and paying attention, opportunities will pass us by and we will miss out on the important things in life. If that left hook comes and you're unprepared, chances are you won't be able to duck or get your mitt up in time to block it. When someone is physically throwing punches at your face – even in training – it can be the impetus needed to wake up and ready yourself for what lies ahead.

Before each round, my coach calls out combinations numerically. "1, 2, 3, 6, 3, 5." He is denoting the sequential pattern of the type of punches we are to throw. He will often provide a visual demonstration for us to follow. Within our partnership, it is our responsibility to memorize the combination and then to execute it accurately with our partner. If we fail to do this, either the mitt holder or the person throwing the punches can end up with an injury. So, if we are not alert and miss the directives from our coach, we jeopardize the safety of both people in the partnership. For this reason, it is unfair to yourself or to one's partner not to pay attention; just as it is also inappropriate to risk injury through negligence. 1 Peter 5:8 makes this abundantly clear: *"Be alert and of sober mind. Your enemy, the devil prowls around like a roaring lion looking for someone to devour."*

My advice in response is this: Do not enter the boxing ring of life with a bad attitude. Do not always be the first to throw a punch, and know when you are about to receive one. Even if all odds are stacked against you, step up and step out. Put your guard up and be ready. Be alert. Listen well. Duck when necessary and deflect when needed, but don't give up on yourself or fail to enter the round ahead. If you are not distracted, you can more easily perceive expectations and you are much less likely to be disappointed by the outcome of your actions or circumstances. And when you are aware of God's presence in your life, you can maintain a strong guard against that which seeks to divert you from Him.

Let your eyes look straight ahead; fix your gaze on what lies before you. Give careful thought to the paths for your feet and be steadfast in all your ways. Do not turn to the right or the left; keep your foot from evil (Proverbs 4:25-27).

TRAIN. CONNECT. PRAY.

How will you **train** for Christ and His Kingdom today?
How will you **connect** with others today?
How will you **pray** today?

DEVOTIONAL INQUIRY:

1. **Train:** What resonated with you from this section about "Disappointment and Distraction?"

   _____

   _____

   _____

2. **Connect:** How does this message connect to your own personal disappointments? What distractions in your life keep you from pursuing God's purpose for your life?

   _____

   _____

   _____

3. **Pray:** How will you pray today? What is the conversation you need to be having with God?

   _____

   _____

   _____

DATE: _____

GRACE IN RESILIENCE SCALE (1-10): _____

OUTLINE your action plan for _prayer, connection_, and _training_ in relation to "Disappointment & Distraction."

   _____

   _____

   _____

Devotional Prayer

Heavenly Father,

Thank you for this life you have given me. I know you did not create me to live a distracted life. I know I was created in your image to live life infected by your love. Forgive me for the ways in which I have fallen short of living by your word and your example. Forgive me for allowing distractions to act as idols before my study of the word and relationship with you.

Lord, please help me to be mindful of the noise and distractions of this world so I can still hear your voice. I know you are still speaking and I need to do a better job of listening. Temptations will inevitably come my way, but I will do my best to resist that which does not further glorify you, spread the Gospel, or serve your kingdom.

When I am disappointed in myself or others, please help me look to you. When I lose hope, I will be reminded of your grace. And when I am in the midst of challenge, I will remain steadfast and fix my gaze upon you and your abounding love.

In your holy name, I pray.

Amen.

Eternally Obedient

"Be obedient," I told my high school English students at the beginning of the school year. "Be obedient. Follow the rules and adhere to the syllabus. If you do so, you will succeed in this class." As expected, some students laughed at my call to obedience while others feverishly began taking notes. As I continued to explain to my students the reason for having rules, a syllabus, and daily homework assignments, I remained surprised by those who still chose to disobey. I had created a plan of action for them that when followed, would lead to their ability to excel in the class. So, why would a student not choose to follow it? Was it mere apathy or was something else preventing them from acting responsibly? After all, obedience to the plan of action would equate to discipline in their studies, and the two combined would provide an opportunity for achievement within the class.

Likewise, when I coach a client through a personal training session, their willingness to be obedient to the plan I have set forth for them often yields stronger results than those clients who remain stubbornly disobedient. As a child growing up with two headstrong parents, I learned early on the importance of being respectful and obedient to both my mother and father at all times. As a citizen, I am expected to be obedient to the rules of my town. As an automobile driver, I must obey the rules of the road. At my workplace, I must be obedient to my boss and the obligations set forth for me. And in my walk with Christ, I am called to be obedient to His will at all times.

The primary difference, however, between my obedience to things in life versus my obedience to Christ is that my obedience in the present moment on earth is temporary, whereas, my obedience to and for Christ is eternal. Eternal obedience is having an understanding and respect for the fact that our obedience to God is not just for now, for this moment. Our obedience to God is for eternity and it has to start now. We have to actively and intentionally practice obedience every single day. We must be aware of the work God has set forth for us and follow it through to completion. Our eternal obedience is not a "sometimes" kind of behavior. It is an "always" and "intentional" way of being. Obedience for the sake of eternity shows our acceptance of our chosen life in Christ.

Why do we so often think in the fashion of my English students, that it is okay to only obey God when it is convenient or comfortable? Do we have an expectation about some guarantee of eternal life that permits us to behave in ways that don't honor Christ? While it may be okay to disobey a boss for the sake of safety or protection of personal well-being, there is never a time when it is okay to disobey Christ. He sacrificed himself for our freedom to live in Him and for Him, not to stand up against Him. We must consider what it is in this life that has eternal value. How is God glorified through our actions?

Remember that with each challenge you face, you have a choice to either walk away from God or submit to Him. In your submission, you receive the gift of eternal citizenship. The power of eternal obedience is furthered when we turn to Him for freedom from our fleshly bondages on Earth. The embodiment of an eternal mindset allows God to actively work in us so that we may come to more fully believe in His ultimate sovereignty. Our deliberate and fearless obedience to Christ secures His eternal glory.

RUNNING & REAPING

*What are you running towards
in your life, no matter how hard
the race becomes?*

"Are you running to or are you running from?" That is the question the nurse at my high school asked me as I rested in her office between classes. My body was too feeble to rise up and respond. Everyone seemed to know about my affliction with anorexia, but me. Peers and teachers recognized my illness. My parents were begging me to go to counseling, but I not yet admitted that I had any kind of problem. I was not, in any way, willing to give in to accepting the label of being "anorexic." I was a junior in high school. My friendships had dwindled as a result of my retreat from social activities. I quit participation in sports and music and I poured my remaining energy into maintaining straight A's. I had transferred high schools, never dated and at 17 years old, I had never been kissed.

"Are you running to or are you running from?" The question still echoes in my mind today as it did in my junior year of high school. The only difference is that now I work to confront the question rather than avoiding it. In high school, I was most certainly running. I was running from my fear of self, others, and from my very own life. As a grown adult, I have encountered many moments when I still wanted to run away from work, responsibility, and relationships.

"Are you running to or are you running from?" The temptation will always be to run from because that seems the path of least resistance. But if that's the course we repeatedly choose, we will always be running. We will always feel chased by our own problems and fears. However, if we

choose to run to them and through them, we can and we will learn to own them and to control them.

As a slated or stated introvert, or simply – As an introvert, through and through, learning to run to and through my fears in the past ten years of my life has resulted in becoming a public speaker, teacher, and fitness trainer. It meant finally having that first kiss. It enabled me to become an author, too, despite the constant stream of rejections I initially received. This layer of running fearlessly has meant learning how to invite love into my life and how to be graceful and selfless in receiving and returning that love. Running towards instead of running away means finding fulfillment in being able to challenge boundaries in your life and re-assess norms. So, run to it – whatever "it" constitutes in your life at this moment - and run through it, because you can be the leader of your own life the other side where you can set your pace and find your stride.

WRITE FROM THE HEART:
Pursuing your Passion

Several years ago, while working full time in a career that left me unfulfilled, unchallenged, and despondent most days, I made the decision to apply to graduate school again, to finish a book, to send out unrefined manuscripts to agents, to stop long enough to observe the world around me so that I could explore the process of creating poetry again.

In 2016, I was still toiling in a job I hated. One early spring morning, instead of prepping for the day ahead, I watched a TED talk by Jeff Sheets called, "Pursuing Your Passion." I watched and listened multiple times to his message. It was so captivating that I shared it with fellow colleagues and my students throughout the day. It contained an empowering message about relentlessly pursuing one's passion through persistence, patience, and perseverance. I had heard similar messages about "passion" before, but I was too scared to commit to living them out. I feared failure and financial distress. As I sat, unhappy and miserable, I realized that I was only writing in the small corners of time I could carve out on weekends. Only when I was not completely exhausted from draining weeks of mind-numbing work. The message that morning struck a chord within me. What was I doing in a job and career I hated? Why was I not trying and failing forward rather than just falling backward or attempting to fit someone else's norm, checking off my life-boxes and depositing reliable paychecks? That day, I spent every minute I could, in the minutes between other things, researching careers in writing and fitness. The TED talk to which I listened, gave me a renewed sense of courage to pursue my creative doing side, the side that often overwhelms my sense of being.

What I have learned after dragging my feet towards heeding this advice is that "pursuing your passion" is not the easy way to go in life. It is not a comfortable, secure route with a guarantee. It is a path you have to forge on your own. It is wrought with uncertainty and fear. There are days where I question myself, I lack belief in myself or want to place the security of a "paycheck" above the patience of persistence in creation. But in the end, I know that chasing a dream or passion is the surest way to bring the most glory to God. He did not create us to quell the desires He put upon our hearts.

I completed graduate school with an MFA in Writing from a program and school to which I never dreamed I would be admitted. My first nonfiction book was released in the fall of 2017 and I have now become a health coach and advocate for faith and fitness. My second book, a memoir, was released in 2018. My first poetry collection was published in 2019.

I do not know what will ultimately become of this pursuit of passion, but I am not concerned with the measurable outcomes of money or success. I have been singing in the shower again. I allow myself to dance into the wee hours of the night. I pray with more intent. And I write - I write to think, to move, to feel, and to send tender vibrations through every last fiber of my heart.

ACTION PLAN:
Running Fearlessly

In consideration of the idea of learning to run fearlessly to and through something, I would like to propose three possible scenarios that most people will confront at some point in their lives. Alongside these are strategies that can be employed to help facilitate the fearlessness that is needed to run to and through rather than succumbing and being chased away one's goals.

1. Illness or Injury

In our lives, at some point or another, we will experience illness and injury. Whether it is our own personal affliction or that of a family member, friend, or loved one, it is difficult to avoid. For example, this past year my mother once again had a health scare and subsequent surgery surrounding her battle with breast cancer. I witnessed three of my grandparents' lives being stolen by cancer, and I have sustained countless sidelining injuries as a fitness trainer.

A microcosm of this? I broke a toe. Yes, I broke my third toe joint and mangled my foot during a summer triathlon. It took eight weeks to heal. I was frustrated and angry that I was forced to be so diligent and patient in the process of healing. I was unable to work or workout. I longed to return to my normal life. I did not want to hobble around and watch my legs atrophy. In my struggle, I learned how reliant I was on exercise as an escape from rather than as a solution to many unresolved or unsettled issues in my life. It was not pleasant, but it was an important lesson to learn. Even though I could not physically "run" in my condition, I practiced facing the injury head-on, not dwelling on that which was out of my control.

In any case of illness or injury, we can run from it or pretend to ignore as if it does not exist. However, that attitude does not promote healing nor does it promote the recognition of the present moment of struggle and what we can learn through the experience.

Action Steps for Illness & Injury Management:

- Be Angry! Be frustrated! But don't harbor a negative attitude. Healing is as much mental as it is physical.
- Accept love and help from others. Allow yourself to ask for it when needed.

- Assess what you need to return to health. Create an action plan and make daily, weekly, and monthly goals.
- Give yourself time to heal. Learn patience and allow the experience to teach you what it is you need to learn at the moment. Those teachings will grow you as a person.
- Don't dwell on the past or too heavily anticipate the future. Be content in the moment of the struggle and practice giving affirmations of love to yourself and to others each day.

2. Death or Loss

Unfortunately, as humans, we have a 100 percent mortality rate. We will not get out of this thing alive! So, in some capacity or another, all humans deal with the unsettling notion of death. We wrestle at times with the spiritual belief in the reality of an eternal life following our physical life on earth. And at some point, in our lives, before we die, we will experience the death of a loved one, a friend, or a pet. We will experience the loss of a job, a home, money, love, or stability. It is inevitable to experience such things. And in both encountering death and loss, we are apt to harbor the emotional distress of resentment, anger, and grief. We can easily run from these things and attempt to fill the aching void with food or alcohol, unhealthy hobbies, or disenfranchisement from our own lives. But once again, doing so does not promote healing or a continued journey of health in any way. At times, retreating from loss seems the only way to get to the next day or make the tears stop, but it does not solve the problem or uproot that cavernous loneliness that is wedging its way into your heart. "Running towards" death or loss sounds insensitive and foolish, but we do need to acknowledge and embrace it. In fact, we become stronger through the often-painful experience of losing and loving again – of seeing death juxtaposed by new life.

Action Steps for Management of Death or Loss:

- Pray. No, do not pray for immediate forgiveness for your anger, attitude, or hostile disappointment with a given situation. Pray with thanksgiving for God's kingdom and your steadfast reliance on His plan for your life.

- Seek counsel, guidance, and comfort in others – family, friends, and church community.
- Acknowledge your grief and emotions – write, speak, and reflect. Know that you are entitled to feel the way you do. Do not make yourself feel obligated to hold on to guilt for the way you feel about death or loss.
- In loss and in death, remember the person or thing with honor and with reverence. Do not hold grudges and do not delay acts of forgiveness when applicable.

3. Relational Distress

Whether we'd like to admit it or not, relationships with family, friends, and coworkers make up a large portion of our life. These relationships can be a primary source of both our contentment and our angst. Or maybe certain relationships we wish we had in our lives do not exist and that, too, can cause conflict, stress, or even depression. Maintaining strong relationships with friends, spouses, coworkers, or family members, however, is not easy to do. It requires acts of intentionality, not just showing up at Christmas or New Year's, but being present all year long. It involves reaching out and reaching up. It means giving up self to better love others.

Actions such as coffee dates, shared activities, praying together, or yes, calling your mom if you still can, are called relational deposits. It is similar to putting money in the bank. The more frequent the deposits, the more the relationship grows. And as most of you reading this book likely know, the more money you have in the bank, the more insurance you have for the times when something goes wrong. The more deposits you have, the more money that is available for that rainy day or to fill that emergency fund.

We need to start by treating the relationships in our lives the same way. We grow them by pouring into them, and we maintain them by depositing our time or energy so they don't become totally depleted. We do this not because it is always an easy thing to do. We do this because positive relationships make us happier and in turn, make us healthier.

A longitudinal study conducted by Harvard University, which tracked the health of 268 Harvard sophomores in 1938 during the Great Depression and followed them through their lives, revealed highly surprising markers of what truly makes people happy. As part of the Grant Study, it was the longest study to date of adult life and evaluated the mental and physical health of each participant as they went through life and confronted the aging process.

As it turns out, the underlying factor that makes people happy is not fame, wealth, or personal success. Rather it is overpoweringly enduring love and meaningful relationships. The study, of which 19 people are still alive to talk about, concluded that the cornerstone component to a happy and healthy life is strong relationships. Relationships that are consistently nurtured delay the decline of mental and physical health, and keep people intellectually sharp. Not to mention, committed relationships, such as happy marriages often lead to longer lifespans overall in addition to improved cognitive, physical, and emotional health.

As Robert Waldinger, current director of the study and acting psychiatrist at Massachusetts General Hospital, observed, "The surprising finding is that our relationships and how happy we are in our relationships have a powerful influence on our health. Taking care of your body is important, but tending to your relationships is a form of self-care, too. That, I think, is the revelation" (*The Harvard Gazette*, 2017).

Furthermore, we also must make consistent relational deposits because conflict will arise, problems will come up, gossip might get the best of us, or dishonesty may get in the way of the trust needed to maintain strong relationships. But if we have built up those stores and if we have given our relationships our best efforts, then the tension that may surface will be more easily mitigated. There's a much better chance for the survival of the relationship despite the unrest. We can also trust the fact that we lean on these relationships when we need additional support as well.

Relationships, in many ways, are like rubber bands. There will always be a tug and pull, and sometimes one side tugs or pulls harder than the other. And over time, without reinforcements, the band can wear thin. Yet, if you continue to add rubber bands for reinforcement, the tether becomes stronger and no single rubber band is responsible for holding the relationship together. Instead, the multiple bands become a collective force that will stand the test of time and the regular dose of turbulence that life provides. So, go! Gather those rubber bands and make some relational deposits!

Action Steps for Management of Relational Distress:

- Know that tension is normal. Believe that love can heal all wrongs.
- Be fearless in standing up for yourself even if confrontation is not pleasant.
- Embrace self-love and remember your worth in Christ. Pray for your relationship and ask enduring strength to weather the storm.
- Seek outside help and perspective when the situation calls for it.

My advice, in the end, is to do yourself a favor and don't let yourself dissolve in fear of an unknown outcome. Trust your judgment. You may win sometimes and you may lose sometimes, but you didn't run away. Remember that. Ask yourself the followings questions as a way to self-evaluate where you are and what action steps may be needed to get to the place you wish to be so that you can be running to rather than running from crossroads or difficulties in your life.

1. What is it that I am currently running from?
2. What will it take for me to run TO this current juncture in my life?
3. How much will I need to change my ways in order to become fearless in life and relationships?

I run in the path of your commands, for you have broadened my understanding (Psalm 113:32).

TRAIN. CONNECT. PRAY.

How will you **train** for Christ and His Kingdom today?
How will you **connect** with others today?
How will you **pray** today?

DEVOTIONAL INQUIRY:

1. **Train:** What resonated with you from this section about "Running & Reaping?" What does it mean to run *to* something rather than run *from* it?

   _____

   _____

   _____

2. **Connect:** Review your answers to the questions above. What connections can you make between this chapter and events or hardships within your own life?

   _____

   _____

   _____

3. **Pray:** How will you pray today? What is the conversation you need to be having with God?

   _____

   _____

   _____

DATE: _____

GRACE IN RESILIENCE SCALE (1-10): _____

OUTLINE your action plan for *prayer, connection*, and *training* in relation to "Running & Reaping."

_____

_____

_____

Devotional Prayer

Heavenly Father,

Thank you for the splendor of this life! For showing me the way of your truth, I rejoice in you! Help me, God, to run towards you instead of away from you. Help me to be witness to your provision and leadership in my life.

Lord, when I struggle with illness or injury, let me always look to you. When grief has me in a dark place, let me remember your light eternal, and when relational distress affects my attitude and my heart's ability to feel happiness, let me be reminded that the greatest joy, my forever joy is found only through you.

Lord, I pray I will keep fearlessly running after you so you know and see the yearning on my heart for you. You have given us limited time here on earth and I want to affect as much change as I can for the glory of your kingdom. I trust I will reap the reward you bestow upon believers when I have wholly given myself up to your leading, the purpose you set forth for my life, and the internal longing I have to capture your love and evermore share it with others.

In your holy name, I pray.

Amen.

Distant & Discouraged

How do you respond when you feel distant from God and discouraged as a result?

About a year before I got married, my husband, or then-fiancé, Matthew, and I decided to purchase a home together. We had both been living with our respective parents, so we had saved a decent amount of money for a home purchase, which we preferred as an alternative to renting an apartment or condo. To honor our faith and the wishes of my parents, the plan was for my husband to move into the home we purchased and for me to join him after the wedding. At the time, we were both approaching thirty years of age and were anxious for independence. We also felt pressure from friends and family who encouraged moving out of our parents' homes and getting on with our lives as a responsible, adult thing to do.

After looking at several homes, we ultimately decided on a brand-new townhome that was part of a duplex unit in a location and city we both loved. We met the builder of the duplex unit and had the opportunity to witness much of the construction process. We were even granted a choice in the selection of certain components of the home such as light fixtures and appliances. We eagerly anticipated the day the home would be completed and were hoping to get approved for a mortgage so we could make the dream home our own. We had both been successful in saving our money to have enough for the down payment and closing costs, but with my pending decision to head back to graduate school, take out an additional school loan, and only work part-time, the monthly mortgage payments for the home we wanted were soon out of our comfortable price range for homeownership.

Anticipating this financial struggle, but both having our hearts set on the home and willing to do what it would take financially, we decided to go for it and make the purchase. With a much more significant amount of money in savings, I fronted much of the initial home acquisition via earnest money deposit and over half of the down payment and closing costs. It was the first time I ever wrote consecutive checks for over $10,000 in my entire life. I drained over 80% of my savings to complete the home sale transaction. To balance the fronted costs, my then-fiancé who had recently taken on a new job, made the commitment to cover the monthly mortgage payments so I could pursue my degree and we could still have a home. The mortgage would wipe out most of his monthly pay. Finances would be extremely tight. It was generous of him to offer this and we knew we both made equivalent sacrifices. We assumed everything would be okay and we would work it out. We were young, flexible, and willing to work hard. However, it was far more difficult than we ever anticipated.

In just a few months after we closed on the home, we were completely house broke. It was hard to even justify spending money on groceries. Gas prices were high, and we both panicked. Even though we were not living together, Matthew was living alone in a mostly empty home. We hardly had any scraps of furniture aside from the bed and dresser he took from his dad's house, a small couch, a chair from my college dorm room, and a wooden kitchen table graciously donated to us by my older brother. We wanted to buy items to fill our home and make it feel livable, but financially we just could not do it. For the next several months, most of our conversations centered on money and our lack of it. I picked up additional part-time work by teaching more fitness classes to the point of overuse or maybe abusing previous injuries and risking burnout. We also started cleaning my dad's medical office during the evenings and weekends to earn additional money. We ate lots of meals with my parents and going out on dates was simply not an option. We had willingly and consciously taken the risk that created this situation. We could choose to harbor a negative attitude about the day-to-day challenges, or we could choose to rest assured that God would provide for us and we would be okay with the delayed gratification of homeownership. Matthew was rather negative at the beginning, mostly because of the loneliness he felt in our empty home. He was getting by with what we had put assembled to make the space somewhat livable. Aside from the shock of the hefty mortgage payment each month, he was not really complaining. He was making sacrifices for both of us to have a dream home *together* after marriage. It was humbling for me to witness.

On the other hand, I was not quite so positive on account. I was dismayed by our financial situation and I immediately regretted the decision that we made. I was still living at home with Mom and Dad while most of my money was invested in a home in which I did not live. I wished that I had my money back. I became upset about the hardship and frustration that now overwhelmed our lives due to purchasing the home. I became increasingly angry. I was mad at my fiancé for agreeing to do this with me. I was bitter that I did not get to move into *our* new home when he did. I was upset that God was not providing for us financially as I thought He would. As a matter of fact, one of my primary workplaces experienced a devastating fire a month before we bought the house. The fire effectively shut the building down for several months, slashing the majority of my income. I did not think God was working in my favor at all, though I stubbornly wanted to feel as though my faith in God's provision was solidly in place. My fiancé's new job was necessary to assure an income for the mortgage, but the commute was horrendous. I had no idea, in retrospect, what we were doing or what we were thinking. Why did we purchase this home? Why didn't we wait? Was this some big mistake? Maybe we did not deserve a home? Maybe the responsible decision would have been to wait patiently for a less expensive opportunity.

I restlessly cycled through all the maybes, what-ifs, and what-could-have-been scenarios, but we had made the decision. We owned a home. It had both of our names on the contract and we were responsible for not just paying for it, but taking care of it. Everything felt out of control. In my frustration, I kept wondering where was God. Had He gifted us the ability to buy this home or were we out-of-line in doing so? As our arguments about finances became more heated, pointing fingers and comparison games saturated the pulse of our relationship. I wondered what God wanted for me. What did He want for us? And where the heck was He? Was this what early marriage was going to be like? Financial struggle and doubt?

The home should have been a blessing in our lives instead of a burden. In my irrational consternation, I stopped wanting to get married. I stopped wanting a home of my own. I didn't want the hardship and I didn't want to grow up and face life. I looked away from God, stopped listening for His voice, and instead, I began to search every possible avenue to make money so I could feel more confident and comfortable. I was greedy but not necessarily for money. I was greedy for comfort. I wanted the satisfaction of contributing to our new home. I made myself frazzled by attempting to juggle too many jobs for which I had neither the time nor the energy. I shamed myself for entering a graduate school program that now inhibited me from additional work. I told my parents that I believed we should postpone the wedding because the associated costs were too great for us to fathom. How could we manage that, too? And pay school loans, car loans, and still maintain the ability for me to chase my dream of writing books and going to graduate school?

I continued to distance myself from God and though my faith was there, nothing about it was active at that time. At one point I became completely despondent. I stopped buying groceries, stopped doing the necessary chores to care for our home, stopped investing in my relationship with the man I was going to marry, and I childishly fell back into the spoiled comforts of living with Mom and Dad. Laundry was done for me. Scrumptious meals were prepared every night. No mortgage payments pressured me. Hot showers were available without cost along with the ability to hide from the world. I could live carefree like this forever, right? I didn't have to move into this new home I had bought and I did not have to get married. I was shut down by foolish, yet paralyzing fear. The remedy was to give my fears to God and trust His hand on my life, but I was not in a state-of-mind that would allow that to happen.

For many months, I was distant from God. I was discouraged by everything happening in my life. We were completely house broke. There was no extra money for dates, or even buying new running shoes for my blistered feet. No money for outfitting our home with the basics like blinds, bedding, or dishware to make the space functional. In my intentional distance from God, I also became distant from my fiancé during this period of financial struggle. I remember my jealousy as I continued to scrape away at part-time jobs, balancing my studies for school by prepping for classes late into the night. All the while, I watched friends travel to exotic places, purchase fancy new cars, and proudly pay off loans. I could hardly afford groceries to fill the refrigerator in the home we had purchased together.

As we approached marriage and our situation did not improve, I began to see the whole picture. Even though we were struggling, I was choosing to be miserable. I was choosing to act like a child. I was choosing to turn away from God, despite the fact that He was there all along, wanting what was best for us. In order for me to be okay with the burden of financial uncertainty, I had to evaluate the blessings in my life. There was the opportunity provided by graduate school, my writing, and fitness – pursuing things I had always wanted – not to mention, pending nuptials with an incredibly loving man. Though I was not observing it clearly at the time, God was providing for us in big and small ways. The struggles we face in our lives are the places where we grow and where God shapes our character.

I distinctively recall one Sunday at church. I was still feeling distance from God and dispassionately praying for forgiveness for my sour attitude. Our pastor preached from Mark 5:40-41. He explained the context, a story of healing, and all of the weariness, hardship, illness and physical challenges with which many of the people near Jesus were confronted. He talked about the ministry of Jesus, his purpose, his healing ability, and his miracles. In one part of the story, he spoke a very intimate phrase spoken by Jesus. He was being ridiculed and dismissed by those in the crowd.

But they laughed at Him. After He put them all out, He took the child's father and mother (who were in distress) and the disciples who were with him, and went in where the child was. He took her by the hand and said to her, "Talitha, Koum," which means "Little girl, get up!" (Mark 5:40-41)

This is a profoundly beautiful image in Scripture. Jesus is present with both this young child and the chiding crowds as a healer, as a promise-keeper, and as a purveyor of God's beauty. He connects with the young girl in a familiar manner that places him at her level. He uses the gentle command, "Talitha, Koum" as a way to warmly invite her to wake up to see him, his goodness, and the merit of his promise. As I continued to listen to the sermon, I kept hearing God telling me to wake up! He was telling me to see His goodness, His mercy, and His grace. Some fancy paycheck was not going to solve anything. However, the ability of my fiancé and I to love God, trust Him, and in turn, love each other, would give us all the strength we needed to work together as a team to care for each other to overcome the challenges we were facing.

Later that same year, during the Christmas season, we would see few gifts exchanged on account of our limited budget. My fiancé and I had both taken roles in our church's annual production of "A Christmas Carol" by Charles Dickens. I was playing the role of Mrs. Cratchit and my fiancé was playing the role of the Ghost of Christmas past. He was a theatrical gentleman but had never formally performed in any production. Eager for his role in his most beloved childhood Christmas story, on the night of the production, he awaited the arrival of his family. His parents had divorced and during his childhood, they were not often present for anything that he did. On this evening, he was hopeful that they would attend. I had contacted them and told them, yet again, the importance of their presence to him. He told me that it was not likely they would come, but in his own way, I know he was praying that their hearts would change. It was the Christmas season – a time for reflection, a time for family, and a time for remembering the miracle of Christ's birth. Why would loving parents elect not to be a part of seeing their child during this time?

We performed the show the weekend before Christmas in the setting of our church's old chapel. It felt authentic and it was fitting for the minimal sets that had been prepared. As the chapel filled with the winter swarm of bundled-up people, cozy scarves, and festive Christmas attire, I peered out from backstage to see if I could spot his parents or one of his step-parents. I did not see any of them. Just one parent in attendance that night would have been enough to fill his heart with the love and support he had craved so dearly or deeply as a child. This was a chance to unravel those bad memories. This was an opportunity for something different. The show began and I still did not see them present. Curious, too, he nudged me since he could not see into the crowd. Without words, I indicated that I did not think they were present. He was chapfallen. My parents and sister, however, were in the front row. He peered out past me to see them. I was overcome with disappointment for him. He had wanted *his* family.

He sighed and blinked slowly, then made a tiny waving gesture at my mom. She acknowledged it. "Hey, look! It's your family! In the front row! I am nervous, honey!" I smiled and affirmed him with a kiss. "At least they are here. It means a lot to me," he said.

"They would not have missed this! Merry Christmas, my love," I returned. As the show began, I prepped for my part backstage. I remember watching him on stage, confident and proud, wishing his parents had been there, but loving witnessing the smiles on the faces of my family as they watched him in this dramatic acting role. My heart was full. He beamed onstage, as though he was destined for the stage, but had never gotten the chance. I could see the juxtaposition at that moment, how our families so differently loved and had invested in their kids. I had been fortunate. My family cared to always be present. I never questioned whether or not I was loved the way he did. He was disappointed that night. While his family did not show up, my family's presence distracted him and also fulfilled the need he had to be loved and noticed. Sometimes, God is artfully clever in the way he provides for our needs.

As the show ended and my fiancé was drawn into the swoon of an adoring crowd, I stopped seeing our new house or the hefty mortgage payments or the cheap Christmas gifts we had bought. Even the argument we had the week prior about being involved in that very Christmas production at the church, instead of engaging in an activity that would bring financial gain was dismissed. Instead, what I saw was my fiancé expressing himself in the sharing of a redemptive Christmas story. Scrooge was a miserable, grouchy man whose heart was changed. The symbolic metaphor of the story was strong for me at Christmas that year. I was encouraged to see him happy, to see him supported, loved, and esteemed. You can't put a price tag on those mysterious intangibles.

What I have learned from this experience and others is that when we become too self-absorbed in what is happening in our lives that might be unpleasant, it is easy to become distant from others and discouraged by life, especially when someone or something doesn't live up to our standards or expectations. In that despondent feeling of disappointment, it feels natural not to look to God for fulfillment or answers, but to look for distractions. If I can find something that will take my mind away from the hurt or discouragement I feel, the accompanying thought is that I won't have to make room for that pain anymore in my life. I will numb that pain and try to remove myself from it. It is a protective instinct to act in such a manner.

In a *marriage covenant*, when someone disappoints, the temptation is to fall into anger, bitterness, or contemplate being with someone else. And when the "*things*" that fill our lives, whether they be activities, hobbies, or cherished possessions disappoint, the temptation is to find better "things" to replace them with. In such a case, we often become immune to God's ability to reward the fruits of our labors in relationships or in things we have pursued. If we can be patient in waiting for them to come to fruition, we will overcome the temptation or need to be gratified in moments of consternation or confusion. Finally, when events or circumstances disappoint or discourage us, the temptation is to give up, blame another, throw in the towel, and move on from that which caused distress, rather than trusting that God will use the situation to better us or develop another layer of resilience in our love for Him.

Examining this temptation and problem of managing disappointment holistically, we can directly look at how God views marriage, relationships, and the events that make up our lives. God sees us through marital discord or mishaps, uncomfortable circumstances or when things in life don't go our way or come our way. It is much easier to become disappointed, distracted, or even discouraged than it is to have faith that God will work everything out in accordance with the will of His purpose. God wants what is best for us and the assurance of his love means that the tangible disappointments are temporary. His love will exponentially fulfill us so long as we continually seek a relationship with Him.

As Timothy Keller said,

"To be loved but not known is comforting but superficial. To be known and not loved is our greatest fear. But to be fully known and truly loved is, well, a lot like being loved by God. It is what we need more than anything. It liberates us from pretense, humbles us out of our self-righteousness, and fortifies us for any difficulty life can throw at us."

If we find ourselves distant or discouraged, let us do our best to be fearless and to nurture disciplinary actions that will assist in remedying it. Do what you need to do to disconnect from distractions and reconnect with Christ. Actively participating in disconnecting from negative influences and pouring into positive affirmation with Christ will refresh your focus, amplify the love in your heart, and facilitate the productive daily organization of your life's mission in service to others and through the achievement of personal ambitions.

Let us approach God's throne of grace with confidence, so that we may receive mercy and find grace to help us in our time of need (Hebrews 4:16).

TRAIN. CONNECT. PRAY.

How will you **train** for Christ and His Kingdom today?
How will you **connect** with others today?
How will you **pray** today?

DEVOTIONAL INQUIRY:

1. **Train:** What resonated with you from this section about "Distant & Discouraged?" How can you actively pursue God when you feel distance from Him? What can you do? What daily, habitual changes to your daily life can you make?

_____

_____

_____

2. **Connect:** Does anything from this passage align with some sort of difficulty you have confronted in your own life? What happened? Did you become distant from God and discouraged as a result, or did you lean into Him and trust in His everlasting love and provision for your life?

_____

_____

_____

3. **Pray:** "Talitha, Koum!" Wake up! Wake up your spirit in Christ and see His abundant blessings in your life.

_____

_____

_____

DATE: _____

GRACE IN RESILIENCE SCALE (1-10): _____

OUTLINE your action plan for *prayer, connection,* and *training* in relation to "Distant & Discouraged."

_____

_____

_____

Devotional Prayer

Heavenly Father,

You have made all things beautiful! Thank you for the love, relationships, and comfort you have provided for me in this life. Thank you for challenging me in the hard times to rely on you and not on myself or others. I praise you for your mercy when I want to give up on living this life.

Lord, forgive me for turning away from you when life gets difficult. Forgive me for wanting immediate pleasure in return for my toil. Forgive me for my lack of patience. Forgive me for all of the times I have intentionally and unintentionally distanced myself from you. I ask that you help me to stay grounded in your word and that I will continue to redirect my ship when I veer into unchartered waters without you.

Lord, you are worthy of being pursued day in and day out. I do not want to walk through this life alone. Grant me the courage, wisdom, and faithfulness to respond to hardships with a positive attitude, prayerful heart, and ready disposition to seek you first.

In your holy name, I pray.

Amen.

Wanting & Waiting

Are you willing to wait on God's timing and plan, or are you wanting immediate outcomes that fulfill the desires of your heart?

Day after day, I am continually astonished by the way God works in our lives to provide for our wants and needs. Oftentimes, the fulfillment we receive is not what was expected and does not match the anticipated outcome that we held. But, it most certainly can be miraculous if we can patiently wait as God scripts our story. How can we practice patience? How can we trust God during the waiting periods? What will it take for our full attention to shift from *wanting* things in life to *trusting* in God's timing for them if they are in fact to come to realization?

One of my most favored examples of being witness to the beauty of God's plan and timing taking precedence over ours is in the passage of my grandmother. My lovely grandmother, the proud matriarch of my Greek family, my Yia-Yia's passage, could not have been scripted more beautifully. While I still like to argue with God that He took her too soon, I know that she did not suffer and despite the grief that accompanies death, our family has kept her memory eternal, a very important obligation within the Greek Orthodox Church.

In my shock and despondency after learning of her passing on New Year's Eve, 2011, just one week after our family had celebrated the Christmas holiday together, I did what I often do to cope emotionally, and I took to writing. I was trying to sort out my feelings, my frustrations, and my hollow anger at the reality of her death. After a few hours of mostly unruly scribbling, I tore up the pages I had filled, threw them in the garbage and sobbed for hours. The next day as grief weighed down my heart even more heavily, I made an observation about my Yia-Yia's death that I had not seen clearly in my utter despondency the day before. As I reflected on the journaling I had done the day prior, I kept seeing the phrase, "washed her feet." I had written it at least ten times. My older brother had washed Yia-Yia's feet. As my mind grasped the image, it began to take on new meaning. I constructed a long poem about her life that I read at her funeral. The conclusion of the pome held the phrase "washed her feet." (If you are interested in the complete tributary poem that accompanies this story, I have included it in the postlude of this book.)

For as it so happened, the night my grandmother passed away before she went to sleep, the eldest male grandchild, my brother, knelt down before her to wash her feet. My brother, at the time, alongside his wife, was traveling home to Indiana from holiday celebrations in Michigan and kindly decided to stop by to visit her at her home in Chicago Heights. Yia-Yia, for a long while, had been utilizing an oxygen tank and wearing support hose and long stockings to prevent blood clotting in her legs. She was taking some medications at the time and she was not suffering from unbearable pain in her body, but she was not comfortable either.

Seeing her discomfort and need for a change of stockings, my brother removed the stockings and hose from her legs, and with a soft cloth and warm water, he cleansed her legs and feet. He took a clean pair of stockings and dressed her once again. At that moment, Yia-Yia was clean, warm, and loved. As I reflected on this moment and pictured him at her feet, looking up at her, I felt warmth in my heart. Of all things in life, Yia-Yia was most in love with and proud of her grandchildren – and in this fragile, fleeting moment preceding her death, she was being graciously served by one of her grandchildren in an unspoiled demonstration of the great capacity we have to love and serve others.

My brother, I soon understood, had prepared her for heaven. The eldest male, in the likeness of Christ, cleansed Yia-Yia's feet and helped her don an impeccably royal purple silk robe before she peacefully fell asleep that night. How remarkably beautiful is that? My grandmother – loved, respected, and cared for - entered heaven's gates with sparkling feet. I still get chills when I reflect on this circumstance of her passing. Of course, it does not remove the sadness I feel that she is no longer here on earth. God called her to heaven in His time, and He made certain she was prepared to enter into its glory.

My grandmother was likely not expecting death to come, but she was not waiting on it either. But in her trust of God and His plan, He prepared her tenderly for that moment. As I go through my daily life, I find the circumstance of her death to be an empowering reminder of the promise God makes to us. He never promised an easy life free from trial, but He did promise we would experience unique beauty through the grace of His endless love for us.

This chapter, as a whole, is probably the most candid of them all, for when I glance at the opening question, I take pause when attempting to respond. In my own life, I want to wait on God, but I get caught up wondering, *how long will I have to wait? Am I even where God wants me to be right here and right now? Is this all there is? Is there more He has in store for me? Is this it?* The moment I become even the least bit complacent in regard to what is happening in my life, I begin questioning everything. And in consequence, I also begin questioning God, which is a very slippery slope to traverse as we try to walk by faith.

The wait is hard. When we want something with everything in us, it is hard when we don't get it. We live in a culture addicted to instant gratification. One of the most popular social media platforms is called, "Instagram." Yes, *Insta*-gram. We want things to come to us instantly. And then we want them faster than instantaneously! We want that immediacy of gratification. We want to feel good and we want to feel good not in the future, but in the now. *We are culturally conditioned to this expectation.* However, that selfish need is not in alignment with what God desires for our lives. He wants us to trust Him and not to act irrationally when we are unable to trust in His plan or wait on him.

How can you find your faith in our "insta-crazy," digital age? Stop counting likes and comments. Stop streaming your life for the world to see. Stop the bravado. And START being a part of the physical world.

Rather than focusing on your digital footprint, put some sincere effort into focusing on your physical footprint in the lives of others, in the eyes of Christ, and the vast realms of this Universe. You are known. You are seen. And yes, YOU are most loved.

Building a relationship with God takes time, and faith develops through experiences that grow and challenge us. But we have to allow God to work in us during that time. We can't jump to the nearest convenience that satisfies us in the here and now because, in the end, God will satisfy us eternally. That is the promise and the reward for life in Him. God expects us to wait patiently for Him to work in our lives. We can't Instagram or Snapchat our love for God or expect to grow in that sort of fleeting relationship with Him. God does not do that to us. He pours into us and has cherished us from the moment of our creation. He will forever love us. We are responsible for honoring that gift of love, valuing His work in our lives, and holding steadfast to our hope in Him.

Personally, I have waited on job opportunities to provide financial and intellectual sustenance more than once in my life. I have grown frustrated and impatient in the wait for what I think I deserve whether that be a paycheck commensurate to my skills or a work opportunity that fills me emotionally, spiritually, and mentally. I waited twenty-six years for a meaningful relationship with a man. I waited another five years after that for marriage. But God provided. And he did so in His time. I waited six years after I had anticipated to finally be accepted into graduate school to pursue my passion for writing. But, not surprisingly, as I reflect on that time of my life, during that waiting period, God was working on my heart. He was shaping me in such a way that my mindset was actively seeking Him, instead of actively seeking all the "things" of this world. God provided me experiences that grew my compassion and made me a more empathetic observer and in turn, a much stronger writer. God knew what He was doing all along. I just failed to see His plan unfolding because I am human in a "right now" culture, and exercising patience is difficult.

Patience to me is a big, fat, "P" word that I do not like very much. I struggle with it and have for as long as I can remember. A virtuous person is to have patience. I know that I have it in me somewhere, but I am awful at practicing it. It is not that I need to have things right here and right now, but I prefer that efficiency and expediency attach themselves to most all things in life. If a movie runs too long, I get bored. If I am really hungry and I don't want to wait for a meal, I am tempted to spoil my appetite by indulging in the closest sugary snack. But adherence to this sort of pace in my life is that which deprives me of the ability to be still. In my pragmatism, I fail to trust the wait and to absorb what God is doing during the waiting periods of my life. Yet, when I can temper myself to stop long enough, I can, in fact, take inventory of all the ways He is shaping my heart and providing for my wants and needs! He is merely asking and wanting me to lean on Him and to trust that He will deliver! God calls us to rest and be still in His presence.

About a year ago, while working on this book amidst other freelance writing projects, wedding planning, and part-time work in the fitness industry, I spent nearly four hours every evening from 10:00 PM to 2:00 AM searching for and applying to jobs. I looked for anything and everything from college teaching jobs to jobs in journalism to gym management positions to entirely new career opportunities that seemed intriguing to pursue. Months passed and nothing came my way. Nothing at all. I did not even receive follow-up notifications on the applications that were setup to have automated rejection or acceptance responses! I kept praying to God asking what He wanted for my life. I was happy with the fitness and writing work I was invested in at the time, but I knew the reality was that I needed to make more money if I was going to be able to support myself and a future family, to afford house payments, loan repayments, and all of the other inconvenient costs of living. But I was anxious, I was lost, I was not trusting God, and I was hardly willing to wait. No job offers. More applications. More months passed and God was merely telling me to trust Him. What I learned during this time of frustration and self-doubt was that a job is not the answer to everything. Money is not the answer to everything. And more importantly, if I am always impatiently waiting for God to do things in my life, I am not appreciating or even acknowledging the here and now of the present moment I should be contentedly resting in. He provided for this very moment, too. And He will provide for the future, unseen ones as well.

Regardless of knowing this, sometimes it is harder to have patience than others. We may patiently wait for a young child to wake from a nap because the peace of their rest has a splendor all its own. We may calmly wait for the sun to rise or the sun to set. There's an ethereal magnificence there we don't want to miss. But, nevertheless, we impatiently wait for our paycheck to come, finances to resolve themselves, test results to arrive, food to warm, friends or family to reach out, or our life purpose to reveal itself. Wanting something and waiting for it is something we learn as a child. And although it seems children are awfully impatient with their needs, I think the older people get, the less patience they tend to exhibit. I can aptly admit that time and time again when I am wanting something, I realize that I am not all that willing to wait for it. Perhaps this is the fault of a driven mind that can't find quiet. Maybe it is because I am hard-wired for work and stress. Or more likely, if I display these tendencies, is it because I struggle with waiting because I wrestle with trusting God? I could also blame society for this mindset, but this enduring need for the "want" in the "now" is my own and it is an area that I am working to remedy through God's grace and mercy.

God has shown me, however, that when I willingly wait on Him, he does indeed provide. For example, despite many years of waiting for writing opportunities and receiving countless rejections, I was finally accepted to the graduate school of my dreams and pursued an MFA in Writing. Much of the content for my final graduate school thesis contained spiritual writing, poetry, and research; I ultimately graduated with high honors. It was worth the wait. After leaving a high school English teaching job I detested, I trusted God to open avenues for me in faith and fitness. After months of hardship, part-time jobs, and waiting, I landed several jobs teaching group exercise classes, I signed my first book contract and my first complete book about faith fitness was published. I also acquired numerous freelance writing jobs – some with amazing Christian companies, hosted speaking events for churches and small groups about pursuing faith, published a personal memoir, and received a contract to publish my first formal collection of poetry. Amen, right?! God is good! Yes, God is good!

These occurrences validate that if I want things I know God has put on my heart, I must wait for them. God is continually testing me to trust in Him and to wait on Him. My life is not my own. This is something we all must remember. Trust the wait. Remember that your wants are personal, but your hope is eternal.

My final question for consideration when it comes to wanting and waiting is not what do you want, but rather, what are you *willing to trust God in and wait for*, no matter what the outcome?

Wait for the Lord; be strong and take heart and wait for the Lord (Psalm 27:14).

TRAIN. CONNECT. PRAY.

How will you **train** for Christ and His Kingdom today?
How will you **connect** with others today?
How will you **pray** today?

DEVOTIONAL INQUIRY:

1. **Train:** What resonated with you from this section about "Wanting & Waiting?" In your daily life, are you willing to wait for that which you want? Or, do you prefer expediency of actions and results?

_____

_____

_____

2. **Connect:** How do you grade yourself when it comes to practicing patience? Are you mindful of your actions in this regard? Do you often find yourself impatient when trying to trust God and wait on His timing?

_____

_____

_____

3. **Pray:** How will you pray today? What is the conversation you need to be having with God?

_____

_____

_____

DATE: _____

GRACE IN RESILIENCE SCALE (1-10): _____

OUTLINE your action plan for _prayer, connection_, and _training_ in relation to "Waiting & Wanting."

_____

_____

_____

Devotional & Prayer

Heavenly Father,

Thank you for the story you have scripted for my life. Thank you for the beauty that is revealed to me as it slowly unfolds. Thank you for each breath I have been given on this earth to inhale your wonders and to explore the sheer magnificence of your creation. I don't appreciate this life enough and I am sorry for taking advantage of this gift you have given me.

Lord, I pray that I can have patience with personal ambition in my own life and I pray that can practice having patience with others. Give me the strength to live by your example so that I can direct my energies towards things that serve you, rather than things that draw me away from you. I will trust you in the waiting periods of hardship, unease or grief, and I will be mindful of my actions when I feel anxious or impatient.

As it was with the circumstances of my grandmother's passing, help me to continue to see the glory of your hand at work in my life and in the lives of those around me. Give me that eternal focus so that I might not be tempted to compare myself in the present moment to that which others are doing, but instead to what I need to be doing for you. Lord, I will do my best to heed your guidance and to trust in your plan for my life. I will wait patiently, for I want to follow your will for my life.

In your holy name I pray.

Amen.

Rest & Renewal

Why must we seek renewal in our daily lives?
How does this better equip us
to serve Christ and His Kingdom?

THE FINAL REP

Every Fourth of July for the past ten years, I have participated in an annual four-mile race in Elmhurst, Illinois called, "The 4 on the 4th." This tradition has served as my sort of all-American way to celebrate the freedom I have in this country to run without inhibition. Each year I have done the race, my finishing time has been within a three-minute margin of error. Some years I run faster, some years I run slower, but I am never shooting for a personal record. Of course, it is gratifying to beat my time, especially when I have actually put time and effort into training, but I usually just enjoy the ambiance of the race, the warmth of the morning sunshine, and the celebration of America that takes place as runners deck themselves out in patriotic garb and sing proudly of America's character and heritage.

For me, what has been most interesting each year as a run the race and follow the exact same course, knowing what comes ahead, is that I always end up in a position between two groups of runners. Without fail, this will happen usually about one mile into the race. I typically end up running solo, trailing a pack of runners in front of me and being chased by a pack of runners behind me. In this exhilarating and sometimes confusing position to be in, I feel as though I am both leading and following. I generally want to catch the group ahead of me and I want to prevent the group behind me from catching up with me or passing me. It is rare when in this position between groups of runners that one or two runners catch up to me or one or two runners falls back to meet me. Either I will catch the whole group ahead of me, or the whole group behind me will swallow me up. And if one of these scenarios does play out, then after a few minutes, the tide parts again and I am caught alone in the middle. I don't mind being caught in between. I don't understand why I don't usually fit with one group or the other, although I don't mind leading and following. But I do, however, feel pressured to close the gap.

This past year when I was racing the 4 on the 4th, I once again found myself in the gap. As I was trying to keep pace to finish the race in a decent time, preferably under thirty minutes, I could not seem to get myself out of the gap. I kept trying to speed up, but I could not catch the runners ahead of me. I did not want to slow down, so I pushed forward, but I was not going fast enough to reach the target of the runners ahead. I felt trapped, but I kept telling myself that I needed to close the gap. I didn't want to be stuck in the middle until the end of the race. As I pressed on through the third mile of the race, sweating profusely on a ninety-degree morning filled with patriotic fervor, I wondered why I was so compelled to close the gap in the race and in my personal life. What did I stand to gain from closing that gap? Why was I always feeling the incessant need to chase something?

As the final 500-meter uphill climb of the race loomed ahead of me, I took off. I tore through the crowd ahead of me and I found myself lodged in a new pocket between two groups of runners just as I had been before. For whatever overwhelming reason, I did not want to finish the race in the gap.

I ran aggressively and fearlessly with every ounce of energy in my legs towards the finish line. My heart was pounding uncomfortably fast and my reddened face was doused with sweat that trickled into my mouth as I gasped for air. My depleted body moved forward stride for stride. 200 meters left to run. 100 meters left to run. I passed four runners on my right and six on my left. I was making my way through the pack that had been blocking my view and there was a clear path to the finish line. Confident and victorious in my own right, I glided through the finish line completely out of breath, I jogged several feet past the finish line trying to gently alleviate the throbbing in my legs and capture my breath again.

As my heart rate slowed, I no longer felt the post-sprinting urge to throw-up, and the pounding runner's pulse through my head dissipated, I peered back towards the herd of racers still approaching the finish line. I watched as runners who had been behind me most of the race sprinted through the finish line with the same sweaty redness and heaving breaths I had experienced just a few minutes prior. As I looked on and watched runner after runner cross that endpoint, I realized that they all still finished the race even if they had pushed through it at their own pace. Witnessing this, I wondered if it even mattered whether or not I had closed that gap.

Using my shirt to wipe the remaining sweat from my face, I began to see a lesson emerge from my patriotic racing and desperation to close the gap as a sort of gauge of my racing success. What I became aware of was that when we are "in the gap," or in those trenches of life where we fear being overtaken if we don't move faster, we must remember that the grass is not always greener on the other side. I ran right to the very same patch of grass after I crossed the finish line as those runners who came through before me and those who came through after me. It was the same grass – literally and metaphorically. Aside from an arbitrary time delineation between the runners in that race, we all reached the same finish line and it was not better nor worse for the first runner or the last runner who crossed it.

So, what did this mean for my life? Did I not need to be concerned with chasing what was ahead? Did I not need to worry about the forces coming up from behind? I walked away from the crowds to find solitude. At last, I was no longer chasing or being chased. It was liberating. I had, in essence, created a new "gap" for myself and I knew at that moment that in the gaps of my life, I can and should find renewal and a fearless sense of reinvigorated purpose. I do not always need to feel pressured to close the gap. The alone time and independent freedom in the gap are a gift all its own.

Certainly, life almost always dictates to us that there will usually be something we want pulling us ahead, while something behind will distract us or try to keep us from what lies ahead. Yet, we do not need to feel constant pressure when distraction overwhelms or we can't keep pace to get to the next thing. In these moments of lingering uncertainty, take the time for rest and renewal. Don't feel ashamed if you find yourself in the space between those things that lie ahead and those things that rest behind because where you are is exactly where God wants you to be.

Most days I have a difficult time believing that I am where God wants me to be because I am not always where I want to be. While I love instructing fitness classes, it takes a toll on my body and I do not always know if I am helping others, hurting others – as in causing them pain and soreness - encouraging others, teaching others, or finding some ideal way to balance all of the above. When sets become difficult for clients or I am wrestling personally with burnout or fatigue I often find myself wondering, *"Why am I here? God, how are you using me? Am I creating a new gap or closing an existing one?"* Yet as we continue to push through to a new set and progression from the previous goals or challenges from the day, week, or even month prior, I witness the output of new efforts in my clients. And even though I might be tired, my faith in the "why" is most often partially, if not completely, restored.

"The last rep counts just as much as the first one," I told my clients. "Movements that are slow and controlled are better than those that are fast and sloppy. Maintain proper form throughout the set. Give it one more rep if you can. Otherwise, self-select a lighter set of weights. Decrease the load so you can finish the set well," I continued.

Verbal cues are paramount to successful fitness classes as they are to be instructive and encouraging, but also constructive to the movement happening in the given class setting or room. As I listened to the beat-keeping music and I lifted weights in the company of others, my body adapted and I became stronger. With each rep and each new movement, I was breaking down my body in preparation for the renewal period when it would become stronger.

"Active recovery," I told my class. "Make sure you follow this workout today with an active recovery workout tomorrow." I instructed them to take time off of the specific activity we were doing, but to maintain a sense of movement throughout their day. Stopping completely would be detrimental to their results. This mimics how we are to act in the practice of our faith. Sometimes there is more focus or fulfillment in Christ and on some days, disruption creates a lesser focus. But even on the days that we are not performing super-sets for Christ, we need to actively maintain our faith. We are not to turn off God, but to allow him to heal us in the "renewal" period. We must give him ample room to breathe life into our beings.

During the interim of my return to graduate school, I was teaching between 12 and 16 fitness classes per week. I started three days per week waking up at 4:30 AM to teach 5:30 AM classes. My last fitness class on those days would end after 7:00 PM. On the other days, including weekends, I woke up at 6:30 AM to proceed with a similar schedule of back to back classes during the mornings and evenings. I loved doing it – bringing pep, energy, and enthusiasm while pouring myself into others. I did not necessarily feel entirely mentally drained from those teaching experiences; my body was depleted in every possible way.

As I continued the grind, I kept thinking about interval training in a workout. Interval training at its base level promotes the idea that there are work periods and rest periods and if you combine them both in a healthy balance, you will end up with a results-driven workout. I knew this well as I had designed hundreds of interval-based workouts as a fitness trainer. Yet, for some reason, I was not applying the same principle to my own life. If you run for a solid hour at the same pace, you get a good workout. If you run, walk, lift, and rest within that same hour, you get a great workout. But if you run and only run every single day at the same time and same pace without rest, you will eventually confront injury or set-backs. That was the experience of my own life. There was variation in my workouts, but the rest periods were far from the present.

I was also competing in races nearly every other weekend. Overall, I was participating in heavy physical activity far too many times a week.

Silencing my moaning body and trudging forward, I convinced myself that I was fine. I was handling it. I did not need anyone to help me. I did not need to slow down. I could do it all on my own. The toe I had broken over the past summer was throbbing and I still lacked flexibility and balance, but who cares? I would power through and be fine.

Then one evening while teaching a class, the hypocrite in me surfaced once again. I watched a woman struggling through an AMRAP (As Many Repetitions As Possible) set and looking at me through weary eyes. Likely expecting me to tell her to push through it and grind it out through the finish, she looked surprised when I set my weights down and walked over to where she was working out.

"Let me help you lower your weights back to the ground," I told her as I watched her quads and ankles visibly shaking.

"Really? Okay. Thank you for letting me finish the set and offering to take the load," she said.

"We are a team in this. Remember that. Together we are stronger and we can do more. Together, we have that ability," I grabbed her weights, easing her concerns with my peppy, coach-like encouragement. I thought about the fact that on most days I would have finished my own set and then demanded that she do the same. But that was not always the right course of action and with my own legs quivering, I realized there was more to the workout than reaching the max level at the final rep.

As time progressed and I started implementing new strategies to the structure and progression of my teaching methods, I noticed tangible results in my clients. And with those positive changes, I observed that in fitness and in life, there will always be a balance of giving and taking. Of lifting and lowering. Of taking on more and enduring through it and dropping some off when you can no longer carry the burden.

And that is true of our walk with Christ, too. We have the fellowship of community to take advantage of in the body of Christ. It is that community that helps us finish another rep or walk that one more step in our journey. It is the community that challenges us when we need it and lifts us up when we grow weary. It is that community that monitors our intervals and carries us during rest.

Being fearless does not mean I conquer every set of every day. Being fearless does not mean I force myself through the last rep to the point of acute failure. Being fearless means waking up with a song in my heart and knowing that I will try to do my best to help others and to strengthen myself. Being fearless simply means getting up and getting going. Moving forward and moving on. Moving backward and not having fear of regret.

Being fearless means active recovery and rest is okay and I no longer fear that which I was once afraid of. And most of the time it is as simple as one more repetition *with a partner*, one more prayer *with a friend*, and one more opportunity *in the company of others* to try, to trust, and to love.

I desire to get to that final rep of life with good form. I want to get there with strength and confidence. Perhaps the weight and burden I carry will be far lighter and my spirits much higher than they are at the current stage of my life. But either way, I want to finish the set with good posture, with renewed strength, and with a most fearless sense of purpose towards the eternal Kingdom of Heaven.

For Christ also suffered once for sins, the righteous for the unrighteous, to bring you to God. He was put to death in the body but made alive in the spirit (1 Peter 3:18).

TRAIN. CONNECT. PRAY.

How will you **train** for Christ and His Kingdom today?
How will you **connect** with others today?
How will you **pray** today?

DEVOTIONAL INQUIRY:

1. **Train:** What resonated with you from this section about "Rest & Renewal?" How does God heal you mentally, emotionally, and physically in the rest period?

_____

_____

_____

2. **Connect:** How will you connect this message or your experiences to help and serve others? How does God act in those reps to strengthen you?

_____

_____

_____

3. **Pray:** How will you pray today? What is the conversation you need to be having with God?

_____

_____

_____

DATE: _____

GRACE IN RESILIENCE SCALE (1-10): _____

OUTLINE your action plan for *prayer, connection*, and *training* in relation to "Rest & Renewal."

_____

_____

_____

Devotional Prayer

Heavenly Father,

Thank you for giving me rest when I need it. Thank you for inviting me to take that rest peacefully with you. I pray that I will respect myself enough to stop, listen, and recover my body and my mind when required, and also when I cannot justify stepping away from responsibilities or personal obligations.

Lord, teach me how to be mindful when it comes to renewing my body and mind. Allow me to be selfish enough that I may break away from others when I need spiritual restoration. Remind me to act in the way of Jesus as he often spent time in solitude, distancing himself from the crowds and his ministry to spend time with God. Allow me to create this distance so that I may be restored for my own personal ministry in serving others.

Please let me rest at ease in you and for you. Let me be renewed through your affirming love and gentle healing of my spirit.

In your holy name I pray.

Amen.

POSTLUDE

Closing Scripture for Prayer and Reflection:

As you conclude your journey through this series about faithfulness and fearlessness in Christ, reflect on the active changes you have made in your life. How will you continue to go forth with a resilient attitude, accepting God's grace in your weakness and inviting the power of Christ to forever dwell within you?

_____

_____

_____

_____

_____

Paul's second letter to the Corinthians (2 Corinthians 12:2-10):

> *I know a person in Christ who fourteen years ago was caught up to the third heaven -- whether in the body or out of the body I do not know; God knows. And I know that such a person -- whether in the body or out of the body I do not know; God knows -- was caught up into Paradise and heard things that are not to be told, that no mortal is permitted to repeat. On behalf of such a one I will boast, but on my own behalf I will not boast, except of my weaknesses. But if I wish to boast, I will not be a fool, for I will be speaking the truth. But I refrain from it, so that no one may think better of me than what is seen in me or heard from me, even considering the exceptional character of the revelations. Therefore, to keep me from being too elated, a thorn was given me in the flesh, a messenger of Satan to torment me, to keep me from being too elated. Three times I*

appealed to the Lord about this, that it would leave me, but he said to me, "My grace is sufficient for you, for power is made perfect in weakness." So, I will boast all the more gladly of my weaknesses, so that the power of Christ may dwell in me. Therefore, I am content with weaknesses, insults, hardships, persecutions, and calamities for the sake of Christ; for whenever I am weak, then I am strong (2 Corinthians 12:2-10).

THE MOTHER. THE MATRIARCH. MY YIA-YIA.

Fragile life on earth
Experiencing God's grace,
Mystery of faith.

A woman of Courage.
A woman of Honor.
A woman of Fortitude and Strength.

She has been admired by many and
respected by all those who truly knew her.
She was the sole, ubiquitous fulcrum of the Cladis family.
In a word of endearment, she's Yia-Yia,
But in terms of her life and her impact –
She's legendary.

To me, Yia-Yia meant many things, but most importantly,
Yia-Yia simply equated just one thing:

FAMILY.

When I was young I never really understood why
Family had to be number one,
But Yia-Yia was persistent in reminding me that a strong family
was not something that you won.

A family was something that you work for, to which you devote your
heart and soul.
And as such, your family does not leave or abandon you,
They'll keep you grounded and in control.
Your family consists of the people

who are without question by your side,
They're an indelible stamp upon your life,
And they give you joy and pride.

No matter what the circumstance,
No matter how far you roam,
Your family are the ones who gently call you home.

Yia-Yia taught me oh, so many things – to cook, to love to learn,
but the most vital thing she taught me is
that family must remain at the center;
they're the ones for which you yearn.

Our presence was demanded – holidays, weddings, birthdays,
And now here our entire family stands unbroken,
giving JOY for her life this day.

Purple was Yia-Yia's treasured color; she cherished its royalty,
Though whenever she spoke of family, she called for steadfast loyalty.
Renascent and creative, Yia-Yia was marked by her aplomb,
But now in striving to be like her;
failure comes and my memories leave me numb.

I told her I got another 'A' in college
during one of our beloved weekly chats,
And she said, "Of course you did, I expect no less,
you're an intelligent woman,
I've never questioned that."
"Andrea, I know you'll go places, my dear.
You work very hard just like your father and Papou and for that,
I guarantee the reward will one day come near."

When I graduated college with honors and a 4.0,
there was no big congratulations from
Yia-Yia, she just modestly said, "See. I told you so."

She never allowed me to feel sorry for myself,
She'd tell me straight and she refused to let me fear:
"Believe in yourself. I know you'll be great," she said.

"You're my granddaughter and there's
absolutely *nothing* that a Cladis can't conquer."

I will not erase the memories.
I will not ignore the past.
Though Yia-Yia's compassion, her dedication, her prescient ways
may slowly fade, I assure you, they will last.

When informed of Yia-Yia's passing, I was completely bewildered and
lugubrious tones overwhelmed my ears, but now in the slow days after,
God's plan has become more clear.
For on the night she died, just before she went to sleep,
My brother, the eldest male grandchild, knelt down to wash her feet.
He showed her that he loved her,
He demonstrated grace –
And of this I am certain, he handled her with care.

This image has stuck with me as tears flood my days and nights – I see
that God has blessed our family at all times –
through triumphs, tribulations and the occasional, undue fights.

Yia-Yia's first grandchild and his wife were there,
They stopped to visit as they were passing through,
Selfless and kneeling at her feet,
preparing her with alacrity and mercy, too.

Visions of this evening have brought a calming peace to my mind
and in such memories my faith is renewed,
for it's only God's love which defies time.

Yia-Yia's feet were sparkling as she entered Heaven's gates.
Clean, crisp and ready for the glorious eternity that awaits.

Reunited with her husband, and other family members, too.
Someday, we all shall join her, our spirits will reign anew.

Yia-Yia can never be forgotten, though it's difficult to part,
I know that I will keep her forever within my heart.

I cannot change reality.
I cannot question God's plan.
Yet through the strength of family and a fiduciary faith;
Trust in God, I can.

And so we thank God for Yia-Yia,
We thank him for her beautiful life.
We GLORIFY His name
For in *His* time, all things are right.

In dedication to a life most resplendently lived –
One that extended far beyond our reach:

Tassie Tafilos Cladis

ΑΙΩΝΕΙΑ ΤΗΣ Η ΜΝΗΜΗ
MAY HER MEMORY BE ETERNAL

REFERENCES

Mineo, Liz. "Harvard study, almost 80 years old, has proved that embracing community helps us live longer and be happier." The Harvard Gazette. 11. April 2017. Web.

Sheets, Jeff, narrator. Pursue Your Passion., TED Talks.

The Bible. New International Version. Zondervan, 2011.

Endorsements

Andrea welcomes the reader into her own story in this personal and practical devotional allowing readers meditative space to consider God's presence and leading within their own lives. With scriptural guideposts, questions for reflection and real-life illustrations, this devotional is a meaningful and worthwhile 12-week journey.

Rev. Dan Dzikowicz
Pastor & Organizational Consultant
dandzikowicz.com

Being FEARLESS does not come easily, but Cladis insists that with reliance on Christ, we can develop resilience in all areas of our lives allowing us to face our demons and come out stronger than we ever thought possible. Cladis again demonstrates her willingness is to be vulnerable with the reader and her sincere authenticity makes her work approachable and endearing. She freely offers up her struggles and shortcomings as tangible examples to guide the reader through life's many challenges and speed bumps. Given my experience serving in ministry positions, I would highly recommend this devotional for anyone seeking steadfast accountability in their walk with Christ or those simply needing a friend who is willing to tell not the convenient truths, but rather to prayerfully face up to the most difficult ones, while offering meaningful solutions. I will certainly re-visit this devotional.

Ernelle LaCount
Former Children's Ministries Director
Calvary Church

Put me in the game, coach! That's what I felt like saying after each week of the devotionals in FEARLESS STRIDE! Andrea takes you on a 12-week journey of the heart through relating deeply personal themes that resonate with everyone. Each week opens your heart more to Jesus and your own personal growth and discovery. FEARLESS STRIDE challenges you to live the life God has designed for you. Discover and overcome what truly holds you back as you allow this book to become your coach for 12 weeks! This devotional can help you get back in the game and know that God is leading you through any and all adversity and onward towards victory! "Swing away" and bat down all your fears as you allow the fullness of God's grace to impact your heart through this 12-week devotional study.

Kari Scott
Founder of River Fitness Ministry
and Life's Little Blessings Book Club